Big Sister:
A Journey of
Genes and Heart

A Memoir by Anne Martin Powell

For information about permission to reproduce sections of this book,
bulk sales, or distribution of proceeds to nonprofit organizations,
contact: www.linkedbyheart@gmail.com

LCCN: 2012919217

Cover painting by Carmen Ramos in collaboration with her art
instructor at Pyramid, Inc.

Printed in the United States of America
ISBN: 1479131288
ISBN-13: 9781479131280

Passages from this book were previously published in slightly
different form in *The Journal of Genetic Counseling*,
December 2012.

A portion of the proceeds from the sale of this book will be donated
to nonprofit organizations that support research or services to
individuals with disabling conditions.

To the memory of our mother, Joanna Law Martin,
who gave the three of us a joyful childhood

And to my grandchildren and David's—Anne-Katherine, Aiden,
Malcolm, Lilli, Joanna—and those yet to be born, who missed the
opportunity to know their extraordinary Granduncle Bob

Contents

FOREWORD

It is almost five decades since our publication in *The American Journal of Medicine* of what we know today as Lesch-Nyhan disease. This disease, with its signature elevation of uric acid levels in the blood, is related to a family of diseases known since the time of Hippocrates as gout. Lesch-Nyhan disease is caused by abnormalities in the gene coding for an enzyme in purine metabolism. Quite a lot has been learned about this disease by us and many others. Quite a lot is still unknown. We don't know why abnormalities in purine metabolism lead to problems in development, usually referred to as mental retardation. What is even more unclear is how it causes its characteristic abnormal behaviors, so beautifully described in this book.

Anne's memoir, *Big Sister: A Journey of Genes and Heart*, brings this disease to light better than any of us physicians and scientists could. I have seen patients with this disease literally all over the world. We have had some in hospitals for extended periods of time. In the early days, one patient spent almost a year in our research unit. Still, all of our contacts are fragmentary compared to the close experience families have with these patients. This book brings us into the life of the patient and his family in a way none of us could.

The book makes clear the tragic concurrence of normal or near normal intelligence and the inability to control the muscles that permit normal communication with others through speech. Some of our patients have better control of speech than Bob had, but they all have problems communicating. The story of Bob makes him their advocate.

William L. Nyhan, MD, PhD
Biochemical Genetics Laboratory
University of California at San Diego
September 17, 2012

AUTHOR'S NOTE

Rather than a specific disorder, cerebral palsy is a blanket or catchall diagnosis for a group of disorders wherein the individual has difficulty with muscle control and coordination due to damage to one or more specific areas of the brain.

The effects of cerebral palsy vary widely, depending upon the area or areas of the brain affected. An individual with mild "CP" may have only a limp or a slight limitation in an arm or leg, while others may have severe developmental delays (sometimes called mental retardation or intellectual disability) and physical impairments, including difficulty speaking. Those with the severest of physical limitations may be completely unaffected intellectually.

Until the 1980s, when the U.S. government undertook a broad scientific study of the causes of cerebral palsy, the medical community believed that most cases of cerebral palsy were due to birth complications that deprived the newborn of oxygen. Even medical experts were surprised when the study revealed that birth complications accounted for only a small fraction of cases—probably less than ten percent. (UCP 2008) Other recognized causes included numerous maternal prenatal infections, infant brain infections such as encephalitis, and injury to a young child's developing brain, such as from a car accident or bad fall. Frequently, the cause was unknown.

In 1964, when Drs. Michael Lesch and William Nyhan first identified Lesch-Nyhan syndrome (also known as Lesch-Nyhan disease), they were among the first to point to a genetic cause for cerebral palsy. Since that time, a growing body of research suggests that genetics play a significant role in causing cerebral palsy, and that yet-to-be-identified mutations in multiple genes are likely responsible. (Moreno-De-Luca, Ledbetter, and Martin 2012)

INTRODUCTION

A bird doesn't sing because it has the answer.
It sings because it has a song.

–Chinese proverb

Dawn after dawn, my eyes opened and met his, smiling at me through the slats of his crib. We reveled in childish adventure and at dusk drifted off to Slumberland, his soft *ewws* and *ahhs* in my ears. These are my earliest memories of Bobby. We were roommates, soul mates, our dyad circumscribed by our parents and older sibling, David, the planets circling our universe. But at the epicenter: Bobby and I. As the big sister, I spoke for him and performed for him. He was my most appreciative—and captive—audience.

Our physical and emotional proximity spanned nearly a decade. At the age of eight, he still slept in the crib by my bed, still *ewwed* and *ahhed* in lieu of talking, and waited each morning for Mother to change his diapers, carry him downstairs, and feed him breakfast. Then one day when I was ten and Bobby nine, *poof*—he was gone. Off to a special school somewhere in Georgia. Like Santa, he came only at Christmas time. David and I went on with our lives: school and friends, marriage, careers, and children of our own. But even in his perpetual absence, Bobby remained front and center in my life, shaping my decisions, forging my values, fueling a passion for my work. Repeatedly—and tantalizingly—charming my life.

I promised myself that someday I would write it all down for my children and David's, and for their children. I would write about the bling in our kid brother's eyes that signaled an alert mind, about the way he breathed life into our family, made us laugh, and stirred a complex brew of sorrow and joy, anger and love. I would explain how our parents and other special people strived to make Bobby's life worth living, and how David uncovered the genetic cause of Bobby's condition, previously diagnosed as cerebral palsy.

So now, four decades and three grandkids later, I write not only for my family, but for families of similarly impaired children, bearing witness that over the long haul, good things can evolve from the most devastating of conditions. Good and important things that can transform us, like the impetus to reorder our priorities, hone new skills, and forge new relationships, the insight to develop a keener appreciation of what truly matters in our lives, and the courage to insist on what is necessary—or just plain fair—not only for this child, but for others who are vulnerable.

I write to speak out about my brother's rare genetic condition, to depict not just textbook symptoms, but the day-to-day reality of living with Lesch-Nyhan disease. Even medical professionals are apt to focus on this condition's most striking characteristic—the compulsion to bite oneself—precipitating cruel and ludicrous hype about "cannibalism." In fact, the severity of this behavior varies across a wide spectrum from child to child, virtually all of whom are boys. For my family, Bobby's physical disabilities and medical problems presented the far grander challenge. Often overlooked is a characteristic that Drs. Lesch and Nyhan noted when they first identified the syndrome: the flaw in these boys' DNA seems to bless them with an alert and engaging personality, the magical trait that made Bobby the emotional center of our family.

Finally, I write for those who learn that their future offspring are threatened by a devastating condition such as Bobby's. They face a profound moral dilemma, often wrestling with unanswerable questions, alone, and in secret. For them I offer the unabashed telling of my decision to terminate a pregnancy, with the hope that my account may help them find peace with their own personal decision. Like the songbird, I don't have the answer. I only know that for me, my love for my brother did not equate with intentionally risking another iteration of his condition.

My brothers and I grew up in an era when America denied its children with special needs the right to a public education and other crucial support for their families. Our country's public education system excluded a million such children, forcing their families to seek help elsewhere at their own expense and often far from home (IDEA 1981). My family's journey paralleled their journey, our story one of manifold others that remain untold.

Had Bob been born a generation or two later, he might have told his own story, using a speech synthesizer like the one used by the renowned physicist Stephen Hawking. But the flaw in our family's DNA manifested long before the miracle of assistive technology, and so the telling of his story falls to me. No doubt Bob's narrative would have differed from mine, but I tell it the only way I know how—as part of my own.

With David's help, I portray our life with Bob and its impact on our family as accurately as possible when told decades after the fact. I intentionally compress some scenes into one, and change some names for privacy. I confess to using my imagination to fill in gaps about a few trivial details, but every event and conversation described here is true, as they were etched on the heart of a fiercely optimistic young girl.

SNAPSHOTS AND MEMORIES FROM OUR CHILDHOOD (1943-1952)

The greatest human yearning...is to recover the sense of belonging and possibility that attaches to childhood, that ghostly sensation of how things felt when life was most promising.

— *Liesl Schillinger*

The Gawkers

If Mother had choreographed our first venture out in public without her to shield us, I'm sure she would have found a way to prepare us for the predictable stares and comments. But she hadn't. Daddy, in a time bind, surreptitiously arranged it.

Before he'd left for work that morning, he'd motioned Suzie aside, out of Mother's earshot. "While Joanna's out this afternoon," he whispered, "how 'bout taking the kids downtown on the bus and helping them pick out a Mother's Day gift?"

Mother seldom allowed her household helpers to mind us, especially three-year-old Bobby who required special care, but once in a while, in a pinch, she'd let Suzie babysit us.

I saw Suzie slip the bills into the pocket of her white uniform. "Yes, sir, Dr. Martin. We'll go right after naptime."

Thrilled about our mission, David and I helped Suzie push Bobby's chair-on-wheels two blocks up to the Parker Avenue bus stop. When our bus pulled up, we made a beeline to the rear while Suzie lugged Bobby and his chair aboard and paid our fare. This time, since we were with Suzie, we could sit on that far-back bench where the colored people sat. I'd always longed to sit back there and peer out the back window.

Downtown, we walked around the corner to Belk's department store and picked out a sparkly blue necklace with matching earrings.

"Would you like this gift wrapped?"

"Yes, please."

Our pretty, bow-tied package tucked in a bag, we traipsed back to the bus stop in front of McCrory's Five & Dime. Our bus was a long time in coming. Disheveled, tired-looking folk milled around the benches, smoking cigarettes, and spitting in the gutter. I perched at my end of the bench beside Bobby's chair while two women gaped at us. Suzie and David sat unaware at the other end as the chat about my little brother dragged on.

"What's wrong with him?"

"Dunno. Maybe it's polio."

"What a shame! Wonder if his mind's broke too?"

All of four years old, I knew the answers to their questions. He had cerebral palsy. It meant the part of his brain that controlled how his body moved had been damaged. It came from when he had encephalitis as a baby and had to stay a long time in the hospital. The thinking part of his brain was unhurt, his mind just fine, thank you, ma'am. But these grown-ups talked like my brother was some stupid pet or potted plant, as if he couldn't understand every single word they said. I would not answer their nosy questions.

"Yeah, a pity—jes' look at them long lashes."

Clearly upset, Bobby grimaced and turned his head away. Scooting closer, I wrapped my arm around his shoulders. In my head I screamed, *Leave him alone! GO AWAY!* but my lips refused, so I scrunched up my face and shot them my meanest, dirtiest look. Their talk tapered off, though I still felt their eyes burning our backs.

Our bus finally rescued us—too late to salvage my fascination with riding it, but Mother loved her jewelry set. She kept it for years in the jewelry box atop her dressing table, but not as long as my heart held the memory of those rude hags' pity party.

Our Baby Brother

When Bobby was born in 1944, I was fourteen months old. Our older brother, David, was three and a half. I don't recall Bobby being sick over his first year, but Mother said he had such bad seizures they had to take him up to North Carolina to Duke Hospital.

Bobby just home from Duke Hospital. David in his soldier suit.

Duke was where our father had attended medical school and where our parents met. Bobby stayed there for several months while Daddy's mentor and former colleagues watched over him, and Mother returned home to care for David and me.

Behind me and my dolls, Bobby, around his first birthday.

Roommates

Bobby and I shared the upstairs bedroom that adjoined our parents' room, his crib by the pair of windows that overlooked our front yard, my bed alongside his. Each morning when I climbed into his crib to talk and play, his diaper would be leaking, so I changed him—an intuitive task for a four-year-old momma wannabe like me. Yanking the rubber pants down to his knees, I undid the pins and tossed the heavy wad

Bobby leans against my "boobs" so his head doesn't flop over.

of cotton to the hardwood floor. Then I reached for a fresh one, mindful of the need to keep him covered, a lesson learned the time he peed on the ceiling and it splattered back over us.

Hitting the ceiling was one of Bobby's amazing tricks, but his repertoire lacked a few skills that most three-year-olds could manage, like sitting, standing, and walking. He couldn't say any real words, but he laced my chatter with "ewws" and "ahhs," answered my questions with "Uh!" for yes and "Uh-uh!" for no, and laughed at all the funny things I told him.

His eyes, ears, and brain worked fine—I could see it in his eyes and face. Though he was small and looked young for his age, he was neither passive nor withdrawn. When he wanted something, he would fuss at you or stare you down. Once he had your attention, he would look straight at the object, saying "Uh! Uh!" and glancing back to make sure you'd followed his gaze, hoping you weren't too dense to figure it out.

"Is that it, Bobby? Is that what you want?" But if what he wanted was out of sight, well, we had a challenge on our hands. What was he trying to tell us? Who could solve the riddle? David, Mother, and I played this game every day, kind of a cross between "I Spy" and "Twenty Questions."

When Bobby got excited, he had a power surge: his head involuntarily shot back, his arms stretched straight out in front of him, and his whole body went stiff as a telephone pole. If you got in the way, he could knock you silly. One day we were riding in the backseat of the Buick, looking out the window together. Since cars didn't have seat belts back then, I held Bobby between my legs, leaning against me. Mother had barely begun to turn the steering wheel at the corner for the Dairy Queen when Bobby sucked in his breath and slammed his head against my chest so hard it nearly knocked the wind out of me. Ice cream was his favorite treat. When we tried to help him say it, he would open his mouth wide and try to push the "i" sound out.

Bobby's Braces

To help him sit up and stand, Bobby wore heavy metal braces that ran from his shoulders to his heels. Without them, he curled over sideways. Even with them on, his head leaned to one side or the other. "Pull your head up, Bobby," Mother urged a zillion times a day. If he couldn't get his head back up on his own, David or I nudged it back up with an elbow.

The braces were padded with soft calfskin, but sometimes—especially when they were new—they rubbed him in certain spots, making him miserable. If he cried for no apparent reason, Mother asked if he was hurting, and if so, where. He tried to stare at the part that hurt, but we often ended up running through a list of body parts.

"Is it your hip? Your knee?"

When we were stumped, Mother took his clothes and braces off to inspect every inch of his

The braces were hinged at the hips and knees, allowing Bobby to sit.

body. We had to find that red spot before it was rubbed raw and he couldn't wear his braces until it healed.

I was fascinated with the contraption. At night when Mother announced, "Bath time, kids!" I would beg, "Please, Mom, can I take his braces off tonight?"

She would sigh and say, "Okay. I'm beat anyway."

As if working a puzzle, I unbuckled the dozen leather straps from top to bottom: shoulders, chest, pelvis, thighs, and knees. Then David and I would strip to our birthday suits, climb into the tub, and hold Bobby in front of us like cars in a train while Mother lathered him. "Thanks, kids," she would say. "Without your help, bathing him 'bout breaks my back."

She liked to stretch the truth like that. Daddy said it stemmed from her growing up in Texas.

With his braces locked at the hips and knees, I'm holding Bobby so he doesn't topple over.

Bobby's Special Chair and Floor Time

Mother never left Bobby to stew in his bed during the day. Most of the time he sat strapped in his chair which we wheeled from room to room, but he needed to get out periodically to stretch, so he also spent time on our living room floor. That's why David's brown-and-white mutt, Poochie, had to be an outside dog. Mother said it wasn't fair for Bobby to have to share the floor with a dog.

When Bobby was on the floor without his braces, I dragged him around like a rag doll, even put my old dresses on him. His arms were

Bobby's earliest chairs were strollers modified to support his head.

so stiff it was hard to bend them into the sleeves, but I'd seen how Mother rubbed his shoulders to help him relax and rolled him from side to side to pull his shirt on, so I did that too.

I had him all dolled up in a baby bonnet one day and told Mother, "Makes a cute baby girl, doesn't he, Mom?"

She laughed. "Yeah, with a mouthful of teeth!"

Bobby fluttered his lashes like a movie starlet.

"You big flirt!" teased Mother

"Why're his lashes so long and thick, Mom, and mine aren't?"

"He can't rub 'em like you do, sweetheart."

David, age 6 or 7,
shirtless as usual.

Big, Bad Brother David

Mother talked all the time about how Bobby loved me. He *was* always smiling at me, his eyes constantly following me around, but David was a different story. Older and stronger than I, David refused to play with me, preferring to wrestle in the grass with his neighborhood pals 'til they were all red-faced and sweaty.

David called me a wimp and a tattletale, even socked me and got in trouble for it. But I had to admire how brave he was to sleep downstairs all by himself in his room where model planes hung from the ceiling on fishing line.

When our parents slept late on Sundays, David came upstairs to get Bobby and me. We lowered the side of Bobby's crib, inched him over the edge, and lay him across a wicker laundry basket. Then we dragged it to the top of the stairs, each took our end, and bumped it all the way to the bottom.

Bobby never minded the rough ride. In fact, he relished all kinds of rough and tumble play—the rougher, the better. When David or I swung him around, or jumped and bounced him on our parents' bed, he laughed so hard he got hiccups. If his head went "thud" on the hardwood floor, Mother came running with an ice pack. "You're too rough with him," she said.

"But Mom, he likes it!"

Mother with Her Handful

Mother was the one who fed Bobby, a job that required patience and skill. His jaw liked to bite down on the spoon and she had to wait for him to relax before she could pull it back out. When David and I slipped him morsels of cookies or fruit, we took care to steer clear of his chompers.

We were having breakfast one morning before David left for school. Mother was across the table feeding Bobby, Daddy still showering upstairs. "You want orange juice, Bobby," she asked, "or grape juice? Look at this hand for orange, this one for grape." He wanted orange.

Mother's scream made me jump and look up. Bobby's arms were out straight, his head back, and his jaw clamped hard on the glass in Mother's hand. Bright red blood ran down his chin to his bib.

I wondered if that blood was from Bobby's mouth or from Mother's hand. Was her hand caught in his teeth? Or was she holding it there so he wouldn't swallow the broken glass? I couldn't tell.

Mother moaned in pain and her knees

Mother claimed one of her hips was bigger than the other from carrying Bobby around.

15

buckled, but her hand stayed right there in his mouth. "Get Daddy quick!" she wailed.

I was closest to the stairs but too stunned to move. By the time I stood up, Daddy came flying down the stairs, dripping wet, a towel around his waist. David and I held our breaths while they calmed Bobby and fished the glass pieces from his mouth.

No one said a word about what happened that morning, not later that day or ever. Our parents never talked about scary things that happened to Bobby or anyone else. They just took care of it and whisked us off to the next part of our day. But from that day on, Bobby drank only out of plastic cups or through a straw. With the straw, he needed help closing his lips to get the suction going. I liked holding a cup above his mouth, the way Mother sometimes did, and dripping little sips in. He opened up for it like a baby bird opening for a worm.

*All dressed up for a special occasion.
Mother had even curled my hair.*

Playmates

My next-door playmate was Rita Tedder, a Shirley Temple lookalike whose graceful curls framed her forehead, unlike my own straight, corn-silk strands, which Mother twisted into a doughnut so I could see.

(L to R) Rita, her little sister Mary Jane, our dentist and neighbor, Doc Gillespie, holding Bobby, and me.

I loved playing at Rita's house and the way her mom, Janie, trilled songs in her pretty voice, but Mother preferred for us to play at our house so Bobby could watch and be entertained.

Rita was over one morning when Mother had Bobby prone on the rug without his braces. He hated being down there on his stomach—too hard to see the goings-on—but his physical therapist said it encouraged him to work on lifting his head and strengthened his neck. So while Rita and I played dolls, Bobby kicked and pushed and grunted on the floor, trying to get his head up.

His empty braces sat propped in an easy chair like a headless robot watching us. When Rita looked intrigued with the contraption, I took it down and showed her how I could stand it up and make it dance like Pinocchio. Glancing over at Bobby, I saw he'd pulled his arms beneath his chest and pushed himself up so far that his back was arched, his head way up high.

"Look at Bobby!" I cried. His eyes met mine. He flashed a grin and lost it. Down again, back to kicking and pushing and grunting.

Rare time with Daddy.

Our Father

Daddy was barred from serving in World War II because he was twenty-pounds underweight and legally blind in one eye. So he stayed in his hometown of West Palm Beach, Florida, and waged his own battle against the ailments of his young patients.

The war raged on while we were little, though all we saw of it were the bombers that brushed our rooftop from morning to night. The Army Air Corps' landing strip at Morrison Field sat at the end of our street, two short blocks from our house. Playing out in our backyard, we covered our ears as the roars approached and watched the pilots' heads whiz by in their cockpits.

One of only two pediatricians in town, Daddy worked all the time. Besides keeping office hours, he made morning and evening rounds at St. Mary's and Good Samaritan hospitals, and at Pine Ridge Hospital for Colored Persons. He made house calls at all hours of the night and on weekends, but on Thursday afternoons he played golf. Mother said golf helped him relax.

As he left each morning and at bedtime, Daddy gave us perfunctory pecks on our cheeks—his breath always sour from cigarettes—but he seldom played with us. Mother made excuses for him: "He was up all night at St. Mary's," she'd say, or "He's worried to death about that preemie born last night."

Mother insisted we eat dinner together as a family every night, but at that time of evening, our phone rang off the hook. It was always for Daddy, though he never picked it up—Mother's job.

One evening it rang right as we took our seats. Heading for the little phone shelf on our dining room wall, Mother eyed Daddy and asked, "You home?"

He shook his head.

"Dr. Martin's residence," she said in her best receptionist voice. "Is this an emergency?" It wasn't, so she went on. "I'm sorry, he's not here right now, but I expect him momentarily. May I have him return your call when he comes in?"

David and I stifled laughs at the barefaced lie. Daddy lowered his chin and glared at us: *Don't you dare!* Bobby eyed Mother, then Daddy, and began his windup: a quiet little *ewwww,* a couple of staccato *ha-ha's,* then a moment of silence as he drew breath before giving way to full-blown screeching. David clamped his hand over Bobby's mouth so Mother could take the number and hang up. Then we all let loose.

"Mom, you told a big fib again!"

"Just a little white lie," she said with a sheepish grin.

"And Bobby, you 'bout got us in trouble!"

"Boy, oh boy," grumbled Daddy, "you kids are gonna ruin me."

But I saw the half-smile he tried to hide in his shoulder.

Waiting for Daddy

After supper we rode to Good Sam's and waited in the doctors' parking lot outside the emergency room while Daddy conducted his evening rounds. It was hot and muggy with the three of us wallowing in the sticky backseat, the windows barely cracked to bar the 'skeeters. We watched the parade of ambulances pull up, their sirens off but red lights flashing. As the drivers jumped out, opened the rear doors, and pulled their patients out on stretchers, Mother assessed their problems.

"Car wreck," she'd say. Then another: "Heart attack, or maybe a stroke." And another: "Hmm…a bad fight!"

A doctor shuffled out the ER door, headed for his car. I'd seen him at our house when I helped Mother serve hors d'oeuvres at one of her cocktail parties for all the doctors and their wives. Spying Mother, he came over.

"Joanna, how's it goin'? You and the kids been waitin' on Dave a while, huh?" He stuck his moon face in our back window. "Hey there, kiddos. Your ole daddy did an incredible thing in there. Little boy swallowed some bad poison—almost died—but your dad wouldn't give up on him. Saved his life. You should be proud of him."

You bet I was. Knowing he was in there saving some kid's life helped me *almost* forgive him for not coming home every night with open arms and a wide grin, like Rita Tedder's daddy did next door.

The healer and his wife.

20

Kindergarten Without Bobby

Mother would have put me in nursery school back when I was three, but Daddy nixed it because of the polio epidemic. Some of his patients died; others were stuck in iron lungs with mirrors over their faces. He went before the City Commission and told them they'd better stop pumping raw sewage into the Intracoastal Waterway because it was spreading the polio. Soon they began treating

My two brothers in our front yard.

the sewage with chemicals before they dumped it, and by the time I turned five, the polio scare subsided enough for me to attend Miss Reynolds's Jack and Jill Kindergarten for four- and five-year-olds.

Before Mother drove me there each morning, she sat cross-legged on our bedroom floor, putting Bobby through his range-of-motion exercises. She pumped his knees back and forth in rhythm with her song—*Mairzy doats and dozy doats*. His legs made a crawling motion—*and liddle lamzy divey*—though he lay flat on his back.

I stood over them and asked, "Mom, why can't Bobby come with me to kindergarten?"

"There aren't enough grown-ups there to help him, honey. You know kids with CP need extra help. Anyway, while you're at school, we go to Bobby's PT and OT clinics. Don't we, Bobby?" With Bobby's countless medical issues, our dad an MD, and mother an MD-wannabe (in fact, a former X-ray technician), we kids were steeped in medical alphabet soup and knew acronyms like these for physical and occupational therapy or therapists.

"Why?"

"So he can work on using his muscles and I can learn to do his exercises at home—like we're doing now." She was flexing his ankles back and forth and sideways. Then she opened his fingers one by one as she sang, "One little birdie goes out and in, out and in…" He had trouble opening and closing his hands. Whenever he wanted to hold something, I would pry his fingers open, place it in his palm, and fold his hand over it. In seconds, he would drop it.

Finished with their routine, Mother slipped his socks on and massaged his toes so he wouldn't ball them up as she pushed on his high-top, orthopedic shoes. Then she laid his braces on the floor with the pads and straps spread open and set him on top. I helped her buckle the straps, my ability to help a significant source of self-esteem. Mother put his clothes on over his braces, then, with a big grunt, lifted him into his chair, and we headed out to the driveway. Off to kindergarten and Bobby's clinic.

Grade School

Bobby, around 5, proud to be standing.

When I started first grade at Belvedere Elementary, Bobby couldn't go to that school either. With her mind on the following year when Bobby would turn six, Mother went downtown and lobbied the gentlemen on the school board to start a special class for kids like him. (Florida public schools were permitted, but not required, to serve physically handicapped or mentally retarded children, all of whom were exempt from the mandatory attendance requirement.)

David told me she had to "fight like hell," but within a year or two, the board came up with a place way out west of town called Royal Palm School where Mother drove Bobby three mornings a week. Twice a week, a school bus carted him and others across the bridge for therapy at the Palm Beach Crippled Children's Society.

Our family attended Royal Palm's Christmas program where Bobby and his classmates were parked onstage in their wheelchairs to sing and shake the bells strapped to their hands. From our seats in the audience, we saw Bobby's worried eyes search the crowd. By the time the piano struck up "Jingle Bells," his bottom lip was out, his face as red as Rudolph's nose, his mouth aimed at the ceiling, catching flies. Mother went up onstage and wheeled him down to sit with us.

By the time I was due for second grade, our neighborhood had grown like kudzu, exceeding Belvedere's capacity. The school board announced our school would have to go on split sessions. Wanting me to have a full day of school, Mother went before the school board again, this time seeking permission to enroll me at Palm Beach Elementary. That school happened to sit across the street from the Crippled Children's Society where she picked up Bobby every day.

When the board approved her request, she told me, "You have your little brother to thank for your nice, uncrowded school."

The Hillcrest kids: (L to R) Jane Kiel, me, David holding Bobby, Rita Tedder, Susu and Sharon Stewart. In foreground, Rita's little sister Mary Jane, gapes at Bobby.

The Neighborhood Gang

David and I romped up and down the block after school each day, biking and skating with our neighborhood friends, while our moms watched from their porches and took turns slipping back and forth to their kitchens.

Mother usually had Bobby out there in the thick of it. With his fair face and quick smile, the kids warmed to him quickly and were fascinated by his chair and other hardware. When they argued over him ("You already pushed him—it's my turn now." "No, I just got him."), Bobby grinned and lapped up the attention like a hungry puppy.

He took part in some of our games. For "Mother May I," he went "Uh!" to ask permission, and then one of us would walk off the steps for him and move his chair up to that spot. Other times he was content to watch our competition. If we ended in a spat, he'd pout and threaten to cry. "Come on, kids," Mother chided. "You need to get along. You're upsetting Bobby."

We were riding bikes one afternoon when a red pick-up came poking by, its driver gawking at us. As was her bad habit, Poochie chased after the truck, barking obscenities at the intruder. When the driver pulled over and had words with Mother, Poochie looked to be in hot water.

But at supper Mother explained what the man had wanted, her eyes smiling at Bobby. "He offered to make a special trike for Bobby so he can join the fun." The look on our kid brother's face would've lit up our Connie Mack baseball field.

On His Trike

After that nice man came back to measure Bobby, we waited for him to deliver on his promise. When the tricycle finally arrived, our whole neighborhood seemed to rejoice, and Rita's mother, Janie Tedder, brought out her camera.

It looked like any other trike, but for the special high-back seat and straps that helped Bobby sit upright, and the straps that held his feet to the wooden blocks on the pedals. He couldn't actually pedal it himself—he needed to be pushed.

I don't recall which of us geniuses

Bobby, bursting with pride, on that special day.

tied the rope to his handlebars, only that I took the end of it and climbed on my trike, using my other hand to steer. Feeling the drag of his weight behind, I lowered my head and gave it my all.

"Stop! Anne, stop!"

I turned to see Mother galloping toward us, knees pumping, skirt flapping, her face twisted in panic. Bobby had done a face-plant on the sidewalk, his trike on top of him, wheels spinning.

Oh no!

Frozen to my seat, I saw Mother crouch over him, clawing at the straps. Then she carried him, bloody-faced and screaming, toward the house. I'd done a terrible thing to the brother I adored, the one who adored me. Worse yet, all our neighbors had seen it happen. Burning with shame, I struggled to hold back my tears, and rode on down the sidewalk.

Of course Mother knew I hadn't meant to hurt him. She and Daddy just patched Bobby up and never mentioned it again. My recollection of that awful incident was too painful for me to bear—it promptly vanished, as did Bobby's trike.

When the Sun Didn't Shine

The rain had us stuck inside one Saturday morning, playing "Hide and Seek" with half the neighborhood while Bobby observed from his chair in the living room. David, Rita, and I knew not to hide where he could see us. When the person who was "it" approached the vicinity of your hiding place, Bobby would stare right at you and shriek. He didn't mean to rat you out—he just got excited.

No matter what game we played— "Old Maid" or his favorite board game, "Sorry!"—Bobby's presence invariably altered the dynamics. For those who fell behind in our games, he offered a little perspective: *You're not winning this time? Well, that kid strapped in the chair looks to be having a ball—maybe you can get over losing.*

Our friends had to leave at lunchtime because the Harms family had invited David and me to a movie. We stood by the door, waiting for their car to pull into our driveway, while Mother did her best to distract Bobby. But his antennae were already up. He eyed us, then her, hope on his face. "Uh, uh, uh!" His eyes and arms aimed at the door, his countenance flipping like wildfire from pout to smile to pout again.

Mother sighed. "I'm sorry, bub. You can't go this time—but we'll go to the store after our nap." David and I headed out to the driveway with Bobby's vehement protest ringing in our ears.

Well, the truth always comes out: Bobby was no angel. He hated to be left behind, and like any kid, he screamed and cried when he couldn't have his way. Mother would turn his chair to the wall and insist we ignore him, but it was hard. I felt like crying too.

After he wound down, she would ask him if he was finished, and if so, she turned his chair back around.

I'm afraid there's more. When Bobby got worked up, he would do something David and I never dreamed of doing. Although I never caught him in the act, by the time he was three or four, Mother showed me the evidence: "See that dark, bluish spot under his thumbnail? He bit it."

Bobby pouted and looked ashamed, but later we found more tooth marks on his hand. Some of the marks would last all day, and sometimes he broke the skin and it took days for the wound to heal.

Whenever Mother saw him trying to pull his hand up, she would snatch it and bark, "*No biting!*" making Bobby cry harder. If she found a bite mark she hadn't seen him make, she wondered what had upset him. Maybe he'd seen a strange dog down the street. Dogs that didn't know him growled at his hardware and scared the bejesus out of him. Or maybe he'd been thinking about that scary witch we'd seen in the Disney movie.

All we could do was guess. The mystery of Bobby's biting would go unsolved for another decade.

Dear Bob

How are you feeling fine! I'm going to give you a black eye if you don't write me soon. and man, oh man that well be a blackest eye. And I mean it. Have you gone swimming at the Coral Beach Club yet or are you too layzzy When you do go swimming be sure not to swallow any fish because he'll swim in your stomach and you will have a belleach. Tell mother to send me Aunt Pearls and the Mullens N. C. address. Aunt Pearl wrote me a post card.

Love, Anne

Written from summer camp, 1952

BOBBY'S DEPARTURE
(FALL 1952–SUMMER 1953)

While David and I outgrew our bikes year after year, Bobby outgrew his braces. They had to be designed and fitted precisely for him, but no one in Florida could make them to our parents' satisfaction. So every October Mother and Bobby rode the Seaboard Air Line's Pullman up to Baltimore where an orthopedic specialist named Dr. Phelps fitted him for new ones. When I was five, Mother took me along. That morning when Janie Tedder came from next door to drive us to the train station, I knew Bobby was my ticket to ride.

Once I started grade school, I couldn't go along anymore. But I heard Mother talk about the time she and Bobby sat in Dr. Phelps's waiting room and saw a petite lady, impeccably dressed in a boxy Chanel suit, holding a little girl on her lap. Both were brown-eyed brunettes—a mother-daughter duo. The little girl, about Bobby's age, hung her head, sucked her fists, and cooed like an infant. Mother being Mother, she struck up a conversation and learned they were Mrs. Anne Lane and her daughter, Anita, from Atlanta. Chatting about what an expert Dr. Phelps was, the mothers soon discovered both had traveled sans husbands and were staying at the nearby Lord Baltimore Hotel.

At cocktail hour that evening, Anne and Anita visited Mother and Bobby's room. While Bobby and Anita nodded off to the sounds of ice clinking in glasses, trills of laughter, and intimate female chatter, Mother and Mrs. Lane marveled at all they had in common: their families' roots in South Carolina; their husbands' demanding professions; the dearth of services back home for families like theirs; and even their membership in the Junior League where both had gained the confidence and skill to cajole community leaders. They vowed to stay in touch.

The following year, Anne and Mills Lane leased a house in our Hillcrest neighborhood for a couple of months while Mr. Lane commuted weekly to and from his Citizens & Southern Bank in Atlanta. Accompanying them was their son Mickey, around my age, and their twenty-seven-foot Chris Craft, but Anita stayed back in Atlanta with a couple who cared for disabled children in their home.

The Lanes were long gone back to Atlanta on the afternoon Mother patted the seat beside her, inviting me to sit and talk.

"Sweetie," she said, "Daddy and I found a new school for Bobby. It's run by a wonderful couple. Mrs. Gatchell's a PT. Mr. Gatchell's a postman. The kids at their school all have CP. Remember Mickey Lane? His sister, Anita, goes there."

Her enthusing told me her slot machine had spun up three cherries. Well, Bobby *did* need lots of PT. Maybe he would learn to walk there.

Eyes on her lap, she fingered her rings. "It's in Atlanta, honey."

I looked up at her. "But...isn't that a long way?"

"Yes, but we can go see him there and he'll come home for Christmas—maybe sometimes in the summer too."

I remember not one thing about the days that followed our little tête-à-tête, though surely she spoke again about the change that was coming. Her tone would have been cheerful, her words reassuring. I must have seen her packing his clothes, and on the morning they left, David and I would have climbed from bed to kiss Bobby good-bye. Yet I recall no sad moment of parting. Knowing my parents, they played it down: "Just another little jaunt to get Bobby what he needs."

I do recall two subsequent events as if they happened yesterday. The first occurred a few weeks (or was it months?) after Bobby's departure. Feeling unmoored and vaguely off-center, I asked, "Mom, when can we see Bobby again? When's he coming home?"

"We need to wait a while longer before we see him, sweetheart. He needs time to adjust."

The second event followed a long drive with my parents that ended with Daddy pulling our Buick to the curb in front of a modest, redbrick home in Decatur, a suburb of Atlanta.

At the top of the steps stood a smiling, sweet-faced apparition in the white dress, white stockings, and thickly cushioned white shoes that I knew all PTs wore.

"Do come in," said Mrs. Gatchell. "We're all delighted you're here."

I found a seat in the living room while Mother and Daddy chatted with Mrs. Gatchell on a small porch around the corner from my chair. Near me were a half-dozen little kids, some strapped in special chairs, others lying across bolsters or on floor mats. One boy, who was propped up in a standing table like Bobby used to have, kept repeating the same few words, making no sense. The others cooed or drooled in silence. I'd seen kids like this before at my brother's clinic.

Bobby had to have been there too, though I don't recall seeing him: too many unfamiliar faces, too much cheerful, grown-up chatter. Before I got my bearings, Mother stood and announced, "Well, I guess we'd better get going!"

We said our good-byes, marched down the steps, and I slipped into the front seat between my parents. As Daddy turned the key in the ignition, I was stung by the terrifying thought that I had lost my little brother. He'd somehow slipped through my fingers like fine, dry grains of sand. Ashamed I could not stem the tears, I buried my face in my palms and the sobs took over.

Mother pulled me over to her. "You really miss him, don't you, honey?"

My shoulders shook, her words ringing in my ears. *Miss him? Miss him?* Deep in my ribs, a hole gaped and sucked my breath away. I drowned in a sudden torrent of grief. *This* she called *missing him*?

Mother's brief acknowledgment of my tears that morning was all she knew to offer. Over subsequent weeks, no one talked about what I perceived as my brother's disappearance. I heard Mother say offhandedly to friends that Bobby was in Atlanta, but not a word about missing him. While I suppose, late at night in the privacy of their bedroom, our parents may have cried in each other's arms, they believed it inappropriate to share untoward emotions—God forbid, deep and painful ones—with their children.

Their silence reflected an emotional reticence that was common in their generation, although I suspect it was augmented by Dad's upbringing in that tough-talking crew of German-stock New

Jerseyans named the Martins. Whatever the reason, even our openly affectionate mother failed to see that, although her daughter channeled their stiff upper lip, she needed to express her sadness, to know her parents missed him too, and to see how they coped with their feelings.

Suffering my sadness alone, I shoved it down as best I could, while each of us went about our own business. For Daddy, it was the business of his medical practice and golf. For Mother, it was running a family, her work with the Junior League, and golfing with Daddy; for David and me, school and friends. At the end of each day, we took our usual places at the dining table, spread with the same old printed tablecloth, and now with a silent pall. Our table talk fell flat, our faces glum. Bobby's departure had been a dramatic, life-changing event for us all. For me, it was the before-vs.-after event of a blissful childhood.

BOBBY'S HOMECOMING
(DECEMBER 1953)

South Florida's autumn was indistinguishable from any other season, so for youngsters like me, the holidays seemed to appear out-of-the-blue. But when Mother announced Bobby would be home for the holidays, I knew Christmas was right around the corner. One of the Gatchells' helpers would fly down with him and stay with us the whole two weeks.

On the day of his arrival, I felt as taut as the overwound key on my music box. Daddy came home early, his mood buoyant like Mother's. We had a quick supper seasoned with smiles and giddy chatter, and then piled in the Buick for the quick trip to the airport. Through my back window, I watched the Christmas lights in the hedges and along the rooflines fly by, my stomach flipping with excitement.

The terminal was a drab, low-slung structure with small outbuildings to the side—Quonset huts, Mother called them, left over from The War. Across the parking lot and up the sidewalk my eager knees skipped, paces ahead of my family. In the breeze at the open-air gate lit by a single, bare light bulb, Mother pointed north. "His plane should come from over there."

When at last a pinprick of light floated across the black, velvet sky, the loudspeaker confirmed it was Bobby's flight. "Delta Flight 24 from Atlanta will arrive in approximately five minutes."

As the plane touched down and taxied toward us, I leaned into Mother's skirt, the two of us squinting and laughing at the propellers' force, hands on our ears, hair flying. The engines' roar fell to a purr, then silence, but for the tapping of my Mary Janes. Like the ballerina in *The Red Shoes,* my feet couldn't help dancing.

All the other passengers had to disembark first, said Mother, and the men in the jumpsuits had to pull Bobby's chair from the bay.

At last, Bobby appeared at the plane's door, his face to the sky, in the arms of a round colored lady in a white dress. She descended slowly, with Bobby's head bouncing at each painstaking step. At the bottom of the stairs, one of the jumpsuits steadied Bobby's chair while she set him in. Then she worked endlessly on the chair buckles. When Mother finally took a step forward, we all rushed through the gate to meet them halfway.

As Mother wheeled him across the parking lot, I clung to his hand and stooped down to his face. "Santa's coming, Bobby! Are you excited?"

Electrified, Bobby's head was back, jaw wide, chest swelling against the straps, and arms stretched out like Superman soaring through the sky. "Awww!"

Daddy fought to cram Bobby's chair and suitcases in the Buick's trunk while the rest of us climbed in, the smiling stranger taking up more than her share of the backseat.

The days that followed were heaven-sent. I was ecstatic to have my brother back, and enchanted by his caregiver. She was near

Mother and Daddy's age, but she called them Dr. and Mrs. Martin. We all called her Julia. Her complexion was as bright and luminous as an icy glass of sweet tea with lemon. Her dark eyes and beaked nose reminded me of the American Indians I'd seen in Westerns. I was amazed by her girth and the way the sleeves of her uniform strained to contain her upper arms.

After she slipped into a pink cotton nightie in the bathroom that evening, she settled on the rented rollaway in the bedroom with Bobby and me. In the morning as she fed Bobby breakfast, she peppered him with cheerful commentary: "Now Bobby, you better chew these eggs up good so we can get done with our breakfast and ride with ya momma to the store." He locked eyes with her and swallowed most of his mouthful, the rest dribbling from the corner of his grin to the towel tucked in his collar.

All week we doted on him and tossed the same old teases his way. Mother regaled him with his favorite dishes, and at supper, Julia fed him so Mother could sit and eat with us. Before or afterward, Julia ate alone in the kitchen. She was so strong she lifted Bobby and his braces like a feather, and before bedtime, she got down on her knees and gave him a scrubbing—the task Mother had claimed broke her back.

It was Julia's first time in Florida. When Bobby and I took her for walks around our neighborhood, she ogled the palm trees and coconuts, the parrots that squawked overhead, and even the hibiscus that bloomed by our steps. At each of her excited exclamations, Bobby grinned proudly, happy to introduce his new best friend to the sights and sounds of home. That Sunday, Mother drove her to a church in what we called Colored Town, where she spent the better part of the day.

On Christmas Eve, we had our turkey and trimmings at four o'clock, then rushed to the seven-o'clock service at our Holy Trinity Episcopal. The sanctuary, decked in poinsettias, greenery, and ribbons, was so beautiful it took my breath away, and everyone's faces glowed in the candlelight—or was it from the joy of Christmas?

We took a pew up front so Bobby could see, his chair in the center aisle beside us. The acolytes, choir, and reverends floated up the aisle in their red and white robes—*O come, all ye faithful, Joyful and triumphant*—detouring around Bobby's chair—*Hark! The herald angels sing, Glory to the newborn king*—and taking every verse of three anthems to reach their places up front. *Venite adoramus, Venite adoramus, Do-o-minum.* Between reading the words in our hymnals, our eyes were drawn to Bobby, who was crooning in his own special way, "Ewwww, ahhh, oooooh." Every time the organ paused between verses, the whole congregation could hear him, but they just smiled at his getting so carried away.

When our turn came to go up to the altar, Mother stayed in the pew beside Bobby, and after Father Stirling distributed the holy sacraments, he came down to give Mother hers. Then he laid his hand on our beaming brother's head to bless him—the shepherd welcoming his lamb back to the fold.

Santa brought me a new bike and a Madame Alexander doll. Bobby received a toy train station that talked—the first talking toy we'd seen. It huffed and puffed like a train engine, the wheels screeched, and the conductor's voice shouted, "All aboard!" Julia received a new uniform, a bottle of sweet-smelling toilet water, and dusting powder.

The two weeks raced by. Back at the airport, Mother tried to lift the mood by convincing the check-in clerk at the counter to play Bobby's train station over the public address system. She found it hilarious when the whole airport heard the train chugging and the conductor calling, "All aboard!"

But it didn't help Bobby. We heard him yowling as the guys in the jumpsuits carried him, his head nodding like a dashboard figurine, up the steps to Julia's arms.

SIXTH GRADE THROUGH JUNIOR HIGH
(1954–1957)

Like Santa, Bobby came to us only at Christmas. In between, we spoke on the phone, with Mrs. Gatchell holding the receiver up to Bobby's ear so he could reply to our questions and laugh at our teases. She helped him say what he wanted to tell us, such as how he'd taken a liking to some student volunteer or something special Julia had cooked for them that day.

Each year as December approached, our conversation would turn to our plans for his visit home. I relished my annual ritual of searching for just the right gift for a brother who savored all that he saw and heard yet had no use of his extremities. My offering was often some kind of badge of normalcy, like a Daniel Boone hat, or the Roy Rogers watch I got him when he was ten. He couldn't tell time, but he loved wearing what the other boys his age wore.

Each time he and Julia came home, we melded back into a family again, our spirits revived. And each Christmas Eve, Father Stirling would announce, "I believe I hear Bobby Martin back there somewhere. Welcome home, Bobby!" At the end of the service, old friends encircled us while Bobby held court.

During their visits, Julia joined our family circle. She and Bobby were a special duo, reading each other's mind like an old married couple. She kept their cheerful dialogue going, making him laugh, encouraging his cooperation, helping him cope with any disappointment. Seeing the bond between them helped me endure the sad reality that Bobby no longer lived with us, but even I couldn't deny that he seemed to be getting along fine.

I wasn't the only one holding out hope that someday Bobby would come back home to live. I picked up on this in fifth grade, the year we moved across the bridge to Palm Beach. Our new, much grander Sanford Avenue house had three bedrooms upstairs, plus another wing over the kitchen with two small bedrooms and a bath.

"Those rooms over the kitchen were built as servants' quarters," Mother said. "Someday we'll use them for Bobby and his helper. We'll install one of those elevator chairs on the back steps to transport him up and down."

I clung to the inference that Bobby would live here with us. Though I savored the fragrance of Confederate jasmine that permeated our new house, the real reason I loved that house was its capacity to accommodate my younger brother.

The house had a sleeping porch upstairs in the back where we kept our first television. When the picture would cooperate, Mother and I liked to watch *I Love Lucy* and *The Danny Thomas Show*. I also happened onto another show called *The Oral Roberts Crusade*, where the sick and the lame hobbled up to the altar to be healed by Reverend Roberts. He clutched their heads in his hands, squinted hard, and wailed in a rising crescendo: "Oh, come here, Jesus…HEAL, Sister, H-E-E-E-AL!"

Those broken-down people moaned and cried, the reverend crying bucketsful along with them. Believing it had worked for them, the hunched and the crippled tossed aside their crutches and canes, crying, "Oh thank you, sweet Jesus! Thank you for healing me!"

I knew darn well if Mother thought Reverend Roberts was for real, she would've mowed her way right through that congregation, knocking 'em left and right to get Bobby up to the head of that line. But she didn't buy it. When we talked about it at dinner one night, she said, "It's just a cruel hoax on those poor, pathetic people."

Daddy hedged. "Well, medical science indicates there's some validity to the power of suggestion."

Mother thought for a moment. "Yeah, well…Holy Trinity holds healing services, too, every Thursday morning in the little side vestibule of our sanctuary. It's called 'Unction for the Sick' and they anoint the heads of sick people with holy oil."

But I didn't have to wonder why she never took Bobby to any of those services. It wasn't going to fix what was wrong with him. Besides, he wasn't actually sick.

I was spending my third deliriously happy summer at Camp Greystone in the North Carolina mountains when I met a camper who said she was from Atlanta. Without thinking, I blurted, "My brother goes to school there!" As the words parted my lips, I had a sinking feeling, knowing where the conversation was headed.

"Which school?"

"The Gatchell School."

"Never heard of it. What part of Atlanta's it in?"

"Decatur."

I should've explained it was a special place for handicapped kids, but I couldn't—too choked up. Not because I was embarrassed about my brother's condition—I wasn't—but because whenever I thought of him, a wrenching kind of sorrow always snuck up on me, making my eyes well up and rendering me speechless. The unacknowledged ache was still lodged in my heart. That was the day I realized I could avoid those embarrassing tears if I just stopped mentioning my little brother.

But when we were together, I was proud—so sinfully proud—of him.

That December, he and Julia were to arrive on the evening I had a date—one of my first—to our junior high Christmas dance. Too bad, but I would have to miss greeting them at the airport.

Hearing the doorbell and Mother inviting Harvey in, I rushed downstairs in my new powder blue dress, hoping to avoid a scene. David was in a corner of our entry hall, smirking. "Anne's wearing lipstick," he taunted, "Anne's wearing lipstick." Harvey handed me a corsage box of pink sweetheart roses. Nice, but hardly worth the wait for Mother to pin it on while David sniggered.

Harvey's father chauffeured us in their pink-finned Cadillac to the school gymnasium where, in teenage heaven, we all danced the "bop," which I'd learned by watching Annette and Tommy on *The Mickey Mouse Club*.

Part way through the evening, I glimpsed my parents coming through the gym door—and Bobby was with them! Abandoning my partner, I ran to hug him. They had dropped Julia off at our house and brought him to see the teenage fun.

I wheeled him to the center of the floor where we bebopped together. *Do you, do you, do you, do you want to dance?* Every few bars, I twirled under our clasped arms, then spun him and his chair like a vinyl 45 on my record player. My friend Liza, who lived around the corner from us, knew Bobby, but our teachers, chaperones, and not-so-close friends—including Harvey—had no idea I even had a younger brother. Now all their eyes were on me and my cute little brother with the Day-Glo smile, beside himself with excitement, head back, mouth wide, arms so rigid it took all my strength to swing them. We'd danced like this before at home, but never with my schoolmates bopping beside us, everyone belting the words at the top of our lungs, *"...under the moonlight. Oh, baby, do you want to dance?"* The music, the lights, all my friends, and the one I loved best—it was exhilarating!

My parents soon took Bobby home, but that evening of shared teenage revelry had lifted me as close to rapture as I could imagine. My date had been okay, but the real magic had come from dancing with my brother.

Over that same holiday, Mother dropped Liza and me off with Bobby at Burdines where we planned to order fudge snowballs at their ground-floor lunch counter. The instant we wheeled him inside, Bobby's face lit up, his eyes aimed at the escalator. Craning his neck toward it, waving his arms, and saying "Uh, uh, uh!" he left no doubt about what he wanted: *Just this once, pretty please, can't I go on that carnival ride?*

So I wheeled him to the foot of the escalator, Liza trailing behind, where we talked strategy.

45

"Okay, Liza, we'll turn his chair around like this. You stand behind and support it from below. I'll back onto the steps and pull him on…"

Liza's eyes shifted.

"It's okay, Liza. We can do it."

A man's voice rang out across the store. "*Stop, miss! STOP!*" Inserting himself between us and our goal, the man insisted, "You cannot take that chair on there!"

Reading the handwriting on the wall, Bobby let loose with a piercing howl and ocean of tears.

"*Take him to the elevator, miss!*" the man yelled over Bobby's racket. "*It's over there!*"

I had never been embarrassed by my brother's condition, due, I suppose, to our parents' unapologetic example and Bobby's iconic status among our circle of friends. But now his wails had all of Burdines gawking, and it didn't take a triple-digit IQ to see the man was right. My desire to please my brother had almost led me to do something not only stupid, but dangerous.

With Bobby relatively calm once more, Liza and I tried to save a little face by wheeling him toward the elevator, nervously giggling and muttering, "Like we didn't know where the dang elevator was…"

Liza seemed comfortable enough around Bobby, but one day she said, "You know, Anne, I really feel bad for him."

I deflected. "It's okay, Liza. He's happy. He has a great life!"

Truth be told, I sort of believed it, my assessment based on observations from a narrow window of time—the two weeks a year when our lives revolved around him. At the end of one of those visits,

Bobby's howls of protest as he was carried up the steps to his plane had moved Mother to remark, "His problem is, he thinks our life at home is always as wonderful as it is at Christmas."

Dad rarely discussed his patients with us, but at dinner one evening, he spoke of a woman who had given birth to her first child, a baby girl with the unmistakable signs of Down syndrome and heart complications. It was his job to inform her of her newborn's condition.

At the time, doctors commonly advised such parents to send their "damaged" infant off to "a training school" and to "replace it" by getting pregnant again as soon as possible. And if there were other children in the home, the parents would be told, "Think of your other children," as though a disabled child would surely sully the siblings' childhoods.

While I lack any evidence, I would like to think that my father, sensitized by his own family's experience, rejected the misconception that every child with Down syndrome automatically lacked the capacity to be a contributing member of his or her family. But in this case at least, the send-it-away prescription was never issued, because this woman knew what she wanted.

In a reverent, hushed tone, Dad recounted verbatim what she'd told him. "Well, Dr. Martin, I've wanted a baby for such a long time. The good Lord knew what He was doing when He sent her to me. She's in the right place." He stared off into space, his head wagging, lips drawn thin, in awe of this mother's ready acceptance of God's plan.

I was elated by my father's tale. *"Think of your other children,"* *my eye!* If that wonderful mother ever had other children, I knew they'd likely reap the same benefits David and I'd reaped from having Bobby as our brother.

When Bobby was home, he still slept in my bedroom, in the second twin bed (pushed against the wall with pillows on the floor to cushion any falls), allowing Julia her privacy in the so-called servants' wing. Although his bedtime was earlier than mine, he would settle more easily if he started the night out in bed with me. We snuggled and talked until I heard his breathing grow shallow, and then I would quietly slip from bed and tiptoe downstairs where I stayed until my bedtime. When Mother was ready to retire, she would move him from my bed to his.

One night she forgot to move him so we spent the entire night together in my bed. I woke up kind of late the next morning, hearing Mother rattling pots and pans downstairs—so inconsiderate of her when I was trying to get my beauty sleep. Seeing Bobby was gone, I called down to her, "Mom, where's Bobby?"

She came up to explain. "We took him to the hospital early this morning. He was having a seizure."

I had a gauzy recollection. "So that's what it was?"

"What do you mean?"

"I felt him quivering beside me last night. When it stopped, I guess I fell back to sleep."

I felt like a nitwit. Though I'd never seen him have a seizure, I knew he took phenobarbital to control seizures and help him relax. In fact, for years his medication levels had been a running topic between our parents. "He's limp as a dishrag!" Mother would say, or "He's stiff as a board!" as they collaborated to calibrate the most beneficial dosage for him.

Later in the day, Bobby came home from the hospital, apparently none the worse for the wear, and soon, off they went to Atlanta.

Beyond all my focus on Bobby, David and I had lives of our own, especially now that we were teens. While our parents hit little dimpled balls all weekend, David went boating or hung with his high school buddies. Over the summers, he worked as a mate on sport fishing boats, trekking off to the Caymans, Bahamas, or Keys.

Liza and I biked our island paradise, most often on the banyan-canopied trail alongside County Road up to the Coral Beach Club, where we burned countless hours—and our epidermis—around the pool.

Mother was carting me to the club the afternoon she cornered me about a recent bill for our club account. I had indulged in too many ice-cream cones, too many bowls of the vichyssoise I favored with my burgers and fries. "You know, Anne," she chided, "your father works awfully hard to pay for Bobby's school. It's like paying college tuition year after year."

"Okay, okay, Mom. I'll cut back, I promise."

But I resented the curb on my fun. I didn't see any of my friends having to tighten *their* belts. What I saw day after day was Palm Beach's tanned and bejeweled, driving jazzy cars and living outrageously high-on-the-hog. My teenybopper friends and I were already well-versed in Palm Beach's social pecking order. Its upper crust lived off their family's long-accumulated wealth, graced Palm Beach only during the high season—January through April—and belonged to the most exclusive clubs, the Bath and Tennis Club (a.k.a. "the B&T") and the Everglades Club. Our own families came nowhere near qualifying, though we occasionally managed to hobnob at the margins of high society, thanks to a bit of maternal maneuvering. The B&T's ballroom dance classes for teenagers were open to the public— for a certain price.

Our instructor, Mr. Durance, got off on berating his students for their missteps, but it was fabulous fun having the boys vie to be our partners. Not that Liza and I were particularly beauteous or shapely (I was freckled and shaped like a floor lamp), but we knew how to help the boys have a good time. My bag of tricks included making my knuckles pop like fire-crackers, burping at will, and turning my eyelids wrong-side out.

From dance class came a round of invitations to the super-rich's debutante parties, though we'd never laid eyes on the girls debuting. They hailed from Palm Beach's most patrician families—the Phipps, the Dodges, the Van der Whoevers—who resided primarily somewhere "up North" and didn't know enough local kids their own age to pull together a decent sized party. Thus, their parents engaged a social secretary to round up a critical mass from the B&T's dance class.

That's how Liza and I ended up in our off-the-rack dresses with our male friends in polyester suits from JCPenney serving as filler at lavish soirees at the most impressive venue in town, the Orange Garden at the Everglades Club. Those poor debutantes, tugging at their strapless white designer gowns and gloves up to their elbows,

50

looked beyond miserable at their own parties where they knew hardly a soul. While they were stuck in the receiving line with their parents/stepparents, my pals and I fox-trotted to Lester Lanin's twenty-piece orchestra and dined on their sumptuous buffet.

Back on earth, David and I took turns each night setting and clearing the dining table. This evening, our phone rang, the way it always did, just as we took our places at the table.

"There it is, right on cue," Mother said as she headed for it. By now, she'd logged nearly two decades of gauging the urgency of Dad's calls by asking worried parents, "What's the problem?" And she'd developed the habit of covering the mouthpiece and whispering her cursory diagnosis while passing the phone to our father. This evening it was "Pneumonia."

Reaching for the phone, Daddy muttered softly, "And when did you finish med school, my dear?"

A semi-embarrassed smile, then she began passing the fruits of her labor. By the time Dad hung up and joined us at the table, I was blabbing full speed about a girl I'd met whose parents were loaded.

"Liza and I went to her house—her *mansion*—after school yesterday. You should've seen all her clothes. The Capezios she's never even worn, the Lanz dresses, the Lilly shifts—I swear, her closet was packed. And get this: her mom's gonna turn her Jag over to her as soon as she gets her license." I straddled a fine line between my disgust for their gilded lifestyle and my lust for all they had. "Their money gets them everything they want."

Dad's ears perked up. He glared at me and fired: "*Do you believe money could cure your brother's problem?*"

Eyes on my plate. "No."

"Well?" he pressed.

"Okay, Daddy, okay. I hear you."

We finished the meal in silence.

Bobby came home that year for a once-in-a-lifetime spring visit. I don't recall whether Julia brought him, but if so, she didn't stay. His doctors in Atlanta had recommended that his hamstrings be severed. The surgery would take place at St. Mary's Hospital so our parents could oversee his recuperation.

I wondered about the implications of the surgery, but no way was I going to ask my parents about it. It's hard to explain, but asking them for particulars about my brother's condition was roughly on par with discussing the *birds-and-the-bees* thing. And yet, over the years, I'd hungered for more information. Back in grade school, I had surreptitiously perused my father's medical books—immense tomes I could barely lift—searching the indices for terms like "cerebral palsy" but finding little I didn't already know.

Now that I had biology class, I could ask my teacher, "What would happen if your hamstrings were cut?"

"Well, for sure," he replied, "you couldn't walk anymore."

I felt the blood drain from my face. For as many birthdays as I could remember, I had wished on my candles that Bobby would learn to walk, imagining my wish might come true if only he had a little more practice, or sudden insight, or maybe just the right teacher. Incredible, I know, but something like a big sister's puppy love for her brother had made me cling to faint hope until Bobby's upcoming surgery finally prompted my question.

Not long after that rude awakening, I arrived home from school to an empty house. Knowing Mother was still at St. Mary's with Bobby, I headed upstairs to flip on the TV in my parents' bedroom. On Mother's bedside table, I found a letter she was in the process of writing—one of the round-robins she and her family often circulated between Texas, California, and Florida—and read what Mother had written about Bob's surgery: "His legs are so contracted and tightly crossed, it's even hard to diaper him. The surgery will relieve the contractions in his legs. Apparently, this is the beginning of the end."

My heart skipped a beat. I felt queasy. Had his doctors predicted a dire turn? Or was this just more of her usual hyperbole, a pathetic attempt to elicit sympathy from her family? Even if the prognosis had come from his doctors, why would she tell her family (who barely knew Bobby) and not *me*? I was shocked, and livid. Unsure where to aim my fury, I aimed it at the one who'd written those words.

The original seed of my anger toward Mother was my naïve conviction that, as Bobby's primary caregiver, she'd been the one to make the decision to send Bobby away. In retrospect, that was an inaccurate and unfair assumption in light of the fact that Dad was clearly the dominant force in our household. Unprepared to accept such a devastating prognosis and already peeved at Mother, I conveniently blamed her for this bad news as well. Kübler-Ross's initial two stages of grief—denial and anger—held me in their forceful grip. This tension between Mother and me—never openly discussed—would kindle fireworks during my looming adolescence.

At the beginning of my final summer before high school, the director of the Palm Beach Crippled Children's Society, Mrs. Audrey Lester, gave me a whirlwind tour of her facility. I had informed my parents that I wished to volunteer there, having in mind those adorable little kids with crutches and wheelchairs I'd seen back when Bobby attended their clinic.

Dad knew Mrs. Lester well, so he had set up the appointment, but every patient she and I saw on our tour had snow-white hair or none at all. A more accurate nomen for the joint would've been the Palm Beach Crippled Old Geezers' Society. Reluctant to confess my disappointment, I deduced this would be the summer I learned about the not quite so enticing world of adult disabilities.

The big-boned, Swedish-blonde hydrotherapist named Gwendolyn walked me through the steps for preparing the vats of hot melted wax for dipping the gnarled hands of arthritics and the steps for filling the steel hydrotherapy tanks. When she opened the spigot on the full-body immersion tank—the size of my grandmother's Oldsmobile—it thundered so loudly I could barely hear her. Holding up the thermometer tied to the side of the tank, she hollered, "Make sure this is in the blue zone." Or had she said to avoid the blue zone? I was unsure.

By day two, I was dunking limbs and entire bodies in steaming vats and tanks with no one overseeing me. Gosh, didn't they know I might scald these decrepit old folks, or drown them? Gwendolyn returned, thank God, to operate the mechanical lift because our next patient had to be lowered by stretcher into the Oldsmobile.

She was Mrs. Zimmer, a pleasant woman, fortyish—a real spring chicken for this place. She had soft, brown curls and warm, hazel eyes that twinkled when she smiled. But she was paralyzed from the neck down—dead weight in a wheelchair. She arrived in a terrycloth robe and bathing suit. I helped Gwendolyn disrobe her, trying to hide my dismay. Her entire body was scarred and strangely puffy. Her lean, tall, movie-star-handsome husband accompanied her. Both were smokers—he would hold the cigarette for her to take a puff—but the tension between them was unmistakable, even for a Pollyanna like me.

When they left, I asked Gwendolyn, "Why's she so puffy looking?"

"Probably the steroids she's on." Then she added, "She was injured in a car accident a year or so ago. The paper said he was driving but only slightly injured. Apparently, they were arguing when the car veered off the road. They're Palm Beachers and well off."

The latter I'd gathered from her jewelry, the gold that dripped from her neck and limbs, even as she floated in the tank.

At supper one evening, Dad asked, "How's it going at the Crippled Children's Society?"

I assumed my customary dour, adolescent pose. "Okay, I guess. Pretty boring."

"What're you doing there?"

"Filling tanks. Emptying 'em."

"It's all adults, right?" asked Mother.

"Yup. Old as the hills." An involuntary smile slipped out. "Today this sweaty, gross, fat lady came in. One of her legs was amputated, and Gwen had me hold her stump down while she pulled on the other leg to stretch her muscles. *Ohmagod*, it was so hard!" I couldn't help laughing. "I practically had to climb on top of her and sit!"

Dad winced, the pitch of his voice climbing a notch. "For *chrissake!* Why'd they ask a kid to do something like that? I'll give Audrey an earful."

"No, Daddy, no! Stay out of it, please! I kinda like what I'm doing." David had too often called me a wimp. I would prove him wrong.

Twice a week all summer long, I assisted Mrs. Zimmer, her grim tale ripping at my rosy take on life. I had trouble looking her and her husband in the eye, though I knew I should steel myself against the pity—the revulsion—I felt. I hadn't forgotten how those rude hags at the bus stop had upset Bobby.

HIGH SCHOOL YEARS (1957–1961)

High school was going to be a radical change for me. David had graduated and was off to MIT. Like a few of my junior high classmates, I'd entertained the idea of going off to one of those boarding schools in the East. Not that I actually knew where "the East" was. The only time I'd been north of the Mason-Dixon Line, I was five.

Going to boarding school was a delusion of grandeur on my part. My parents would hear nothing of it. "What do you think I'm made of?" my father wailed, "Gold?"

So I headed across the bridge, tiara in hand, to Palm Beach High School in West Palm Beach, the same school David and our dad had attended. Four years before, the U.S. Supreme Court in *Brown v. Board of Education* had required the integration of the public schools "with all deliberate speed," but PBHS's student body remained completely white. A bunch of students in my homeroom were bused in each day from the Everglades on the west side of Palm Beach County. Call me a snob, but their rubber flip-flops—the twenty-nine-cent kind from the dime store—revealed fertile muck between their toes, which offended my Palm Beach sensibilities. The grease in the boys' hair made my stomach roil. Nevertheless, before long, I found scads of college-bound kids in my academic courses, including my old neighbor Rita Tedder, and by then, not even a stretch limousine could've dragged me off to one of those far-flung prep schools.

Bobby was sixteen when, in deference to his teenage status, he became "Bob." In spite of the medical consultations and therapies our parents had fought to arrange for him, the daily positioning, exercising, and stretching of his muscles, as well as the expensive array of custom-made chairs and braces, his abnormal posture and contractions seemed to have grown worse. Sitting in his chair, he tended to lean hard to one side or the other, and he had less control over his hands than before. He could no longer raise his arms to point, except reflexively when he was excited. With severed hamstrings, standing and walking were lost causes. As a youngster, with a speech therapist's help, he had occasionally produced a rough approximation of a vowel or consonant sound he was aiming for—an "i" for ice cream or an "a" sound for my name. That skill, too, had faded away. We kept a towel tucked in his chair to wipe his drool. At the slightest excitement, his mouth would stretch wide, his tongue protruding and contorting his face. He continued to require medications to head off recurring seizures and to relax the contractions that kept him locked up. Despite these setbacks, Bob remained as gregarious and exuberant as ever.

Still small and much younger looking than his chronological age, Bob was also mentally and emotionally immature. And yet, his interests had begun to mature, aligning more closely with David's than with mine. Like any big brother worth his salt, David took Bob under his wing.

Bob was home for the holidays the afternoon I stepped through our front door and heard the ridiculous sounds of "guy" laughter. And

I caught a whiff of something, like smoke. Bob was in the family room, laughing so hard he gulped for air. Tiny strings protruded from his ears. A closer glance revealed they were—*Yikes!*—the wicks of firecrackers.

David's fishing buddy, Jon, was standing over Bobby, a maniacal smile on his face and a lit match in his hand, mere centimeters from Bob's left ear. David crouched in the corner, fingers in ears, bracing for the explosion, while Jon gave a play-by-play of his devilish activity. "Okay, Bob, the left one's lit. *Heh, heh!* Now I'll light the other one."

In truth he lit neither, but how could Bob see that? Was he the least bit worried? Hell no! Macho shenanigans like this were what he enjoyed most and one of the reasons he worshiped his big brother— who yelled from the corner, "Oh no! It's going to blow! Let's get the hell out of here—*EEEYIE!"* David and Jon hustled out to the lanai, leaving Bob behind, tears of laughter streaking his cheeks.

"What are you fools doing?" I demanded, then lost my deadpan. What in Sam Hill would they think of next?

I soon found out.

"Shark fishing?" I asked David. "You took Bob shark fishing?"

At dawn, David and another fishing pal, Mike, had bundled Bob up, driven him to the Sailfish Club docks, loaded him aboard our thirty-foot tarpon boat, and headed out the choppy Palm Beach inlet, three testosterone-revved bucks off to fish the Atlantic. I learned of it only when I encountered the sunburned three lounging in our living room, beers in hand, boasting of their adventure to Mother. Actually, she held Bob's beer—okayed by his doctor to relax him.

On a previous occasion, I had foolishly accompanied David on one of his shark-fishing jaunts, unaware of the insanity I was in for. He and his mate drove full-throttle to a particular coral reef off Singer Island where the creatures were known to hang out and tossed overboard a couple of thirty-pound test lines baited with cut-up and bleeding blue runners. Within seconds, both lines were singing. While I cowered in the stern, David manned the poles, darting and leaping fore and aft like a frenetic break-dancer, hollering to his mate at the helm. "*To port! To starboard! Give it more! Move, Anne—get out of the way! He's running! He's at six o'clock! Shit—he's under the boat!*"

"You took him out to that reef?" I asked David. "Tell me you're kidding."

"Nope."

David and Mike held straight faces and stared at their knees. Bob, incapable of a poker face, wore a proud smile.

"What were you thinking? If that boat had swamped…"

"Unlikely."

I turned to Mother, inviting her comment. A hint of a smile, an elaborate shrug. The message: Boys will be boys.

Oh, yeah, that fraternity-of-jocks thing. So I ratcheted up my outrage. "Surely, Bob, you didn't go out in the ocean with these nincompoops, did you?"

"Uhhh!"

"But Bob, those sharks might've eaten you alive!"

His military-erect posture, the glow on his face, told me that Bob's bragging rights easily trumped the minor risk they'd taken. I was unaware that David had recently shed his dream of earning his living as captain of a fishing boat. The new plan: medical school. The reason: his brother, of course.

Bob and Julia's visits seemed to grow shorter each year. "The Gatchells can't spare Julia for more than a week this time," Mother explained. "They need her at the school."

Julia was an extrovert, a sweet and generous soul. My affection for her had spawned some concerns. She and her husband Fred had no children, but she was close to her nieces and nephews in Atlanta. To give up Christmas with them, she must have sorely needed the extra cash she earned for bringing Bob home to us. I told Mother, "I hope you and Dad pay her well for coming here."

"Well," Mother said, "when we spoke with the Gatchells about it, they asked us not to give her too much more than they ordinarily pay her."

"But, Mom, she gives up Christmas with her family. She works the whole time she's here. She deserves a big bonus—*and you know it*!"

Mother held her calm, that *infuriating* calm. "The Gatchells said if we paid her too much, when she got back to Atlanta she might not show up to work for two or three days. And that's a problem. They depend on her."

I had thought surely Mr. and Mrs. Gatchell gave Julia some time off when she got back to Atlanta. *They didn't?* The Gatchells were good to Bob, but their admonition not to give Julia her due lowered my opinion of them. Besides, what business was it of theirs what we paid her?

By the age of seventeen, I wallowed in a deep murk of resentment against my parents—Mother, in particular. One evening when I stomped off to my room, Dad followed to my door to express his displeasure with typical subtlety. *"What the hell's wrong with you?"*

"She's driving me crazy. I can't stand her."

"Why do you say that?"

"She stands over me all the time. She's smothering me, trying to make me as miserable as she is." Mother *did* seem depressed. Around her friends, she was animated and laughing, but at home her mood rapidly deflated.

Dad shook his head in disgust and walked away.

I could have detailed my litany of complaints, though I knew it sounded stupid and petty. One of my pet peeves was that every Sunday she would wear her gold charm bracelet to church. *O Lamb of God, who takest away the sins of the world*...All through the service, she flipped through the pages of the dang prayer book, her bracelet jingling and tinkling. *Have mercy upon us...jingle, jingle.* I was certain the whole congregation could hear it. Kneeling beside her, I seethed. *O Lamb of God, who takest away the sins of the world...tinkle, tinkle.* When I could stand it no longer, I grabbed her wrist and hissed, "Mother, be still—or take your bracelet off!" *Grant us thy peace.*

Every word she uttered fed my resentment. Too many slammed doors later, Dad came to my room again, this time tossing a threat: "If you don't shape up, I'll take you to *a goddamned psychiatrist!*"

He despised psychiatrists, said they were the looniest of the lot in medical school. Knowing he'd reached the end of his rope, I vowed I would try harder to contain my loathing.

If Dad had followed through with his threat, counseling might have revealed what fueled his daughter's deep-seated resentment, but Mother believed she already knew. She confided in her sister Mary Hart (who would tell me decades later): "Anne will never forgive me for sending Bobby away."

In spite of my recalcitrance, Dad and I managed a few civilized conversations, including one when he asked, "What are you interested in doing after college?"

I'd thought about it some. "Think I'd like to keep handicapped kids in my home," I offered, "like the Gatchells."

He nearly fell over. "God no, Anne! You don't want to do that!"

"Why not?"

"You cannot have a life that way. Don't even think about it."

My goodness, Dad was adamant. Maybe I had better think some more. I had enjoyed working in his office over the summers, but never considered medical school. Years before, when I'd asked Mother why so few women were doctors, she told me it was a waste of money for women to go to med school because they always ended up pregnant and couldn't practice. Besides, I'd fallen behind in science during junior high when our school automatically enrolled the girls in home economics while all the boys took science. I just wanted to work with kids like Bob and knew two other ways I could do that: physical therapy or teaching.

COLLEGE YEARS (1961–1964)

En route to my freshman year at Duke, Mother arranged my flight so I had a two-day stopover in Atlanta with Bob.

As my taxi rounded the circular driveway of the Gatchells' new home, there he was, in his chair, out front, alone, and waiting. Spotting me in the back seat of the taxi, he lurched and flailed so wildly I was afraid he might tip his chair.

Hearing his racket, Mrs. Gatchell rushed out to give me a hug. "Anne, your brother's been delirious with anticipation. Can't wait to give you a tour of our new home, right, Bob? Let's take your bags to the room you'll be sharing with Baby Jane. Julia's in the kitchen, dying to see you."

The one-story brick home, financed primarily by our well-heeled friends, the Lanes, was spacious enough to accommodate a dozen residents, yet fit nicely within its middle-class neighborhood. The interior resembled a freshly decorated boutique hotel—gleaming hardwood floors and chandeliers, extra-wide doors and hallways (to accommodate wheelchairs and hospital beds), Schumacher wallpaper and drapes, framed art on the walls. Anita Lane slumped in her wheelchair before a large, color TV in the oversized living room. Couches and club chairs in a pretty, muted palette filled the room.

Obviously, one of Atlanta's high-end designers had been turned loose on the place.

Anita and four other girls shared a large dormitory with floral bedspreads and pink-and-white-checked drapes. The boys' dorm also looked a bit too perfect. Most typical teenaged boys would have been embarrassed by it, but Bob was puffing proud of his new digs. Mrs. Gatchell pointed down the hall to a suite where she and Mr. Gatchell could retreat in privacy, something they had lacked for years.

My room was a typical guestroom except for the metal crib that contained my roommate. "This is Baby Jane," said Mrs. Gatchell. "She's six years old, deaf and blind—the sweetest little thing." Jane lay on her back, gently rocking her head, which was the elongated shape and size of a mature watermelon. Blond fuzz swept the top and sides of her head like spun sugar, and, beneath the fuzz, was a perfect little toddler's face. Her condition was hydrocephalus, her tiny neck surely incapable of lifting that immense head. I had the selfish concern of a light sleeper: would she make noise at night and keep me awake?

"Where's the kitchen, Bob? This way?"

"Uh!"

Julia smothered me in her hug. "So happy to see you, honey. Right, Bob? Come see our new kitchen where we fix the meals. Beautiful, ain't it? A joy to cook in, I tell you!" The gleaming professional appliances would have done that other Chef Julia (the master of French cooking) proud. "About time for lunch now, honey. You hungry? Here, wash your hands at my sink. Hope you like chicken perleau!"

Beneath the dining room chandelier, we communed with Bob's peers at three round mahogany tables. I was famished, but

Mrs. Gatchell handed me Bob's plate, saying, "I'll let you feed your brother." Mother had always fed Bob before she fed herself. Had she endured the gnawing hunger I now felt?

Julia and another staff member came in to help with feeding. Mrs. Gatchell wheeled Baby Jane's crib into the room and began spooning pureed food into her, while a blind teenager named Claire fastidiously fed herself. Beside Claire sat the school's soft-spoken teacher, Mrs. Pollard, sporting one of those god-awful hairnets plastered to her pewter hair. She welcomed me warmly, but seemed so old and timid that I couldn't imagine her surviving a regular school setting. I imagined her staid personality helped her endure day after day with Bob's peers, who looked to be, well…off in "la-la" land.

Mrs. Pollard gave Bob carte blanche to skip class, so we spent the afternoon exploring the field behind their sunny back patio. Baby Jane was a perfectly quiet roommate that night, and in the morning, Bob and I strolled around the neighborhood. After lunch, we called a taxi and went to see *Swiss Family Robinson*. We laughed so hard in that movie, we both got hiccups.

That visit, and subsequent ones each September en route to Duke, showed me what my brother's life was like—mind-numbingly dull. His peers were nowhere near as alert as he was. His only real companions were Mr. and Mrs. Gatchell, Julia, and the other staff. I finally understood why my father had balked when I told him I wanted to keep handicapped kids in my home like the Gatchells did. No, I wanted to work with kids who had sparks in their eyes, who gave the kind of feedback Bob had always exuded, even without words.

David was already at Duke when I arrived. Like our dad, who was the first in his family to attend college, David had entered Duke Medical School after only two years of undergraduate study.

My first evening on campus, our upperclassman leader asked our small group of freshman girls to introduce ourselves and tell which fields we hoped to study, if we knew. I was the only one who could state my goal with complete confidence: I wanted to work as a teacher or therapist with kids who had cerebral palsy. I had a calling, a true vocation—another perk from Bob.

However, I had neglected to check the requirements for either field, and when I winnowed my choice down to teaching, I learned Duke offered not a single class in special education. I would need to attend graduate school.

Too impatient to wait until then, I scoured the main library's mammoth card catalogue for information about cerebral palsy and mental retardation. Unaware that Duke's medical and nursing schools had their own library, I managed to dig up but a single document: a research study on nondisabled siblings of physically and mentally disabled children—every page of which I devoured. The subjects' experiences mirrored my own with two exceptions: 1) a significant number of the nondisabled sisters—particularly older ones—had been burdened with an extraordinary amount of caregiving for their disabled sibling; and 2) some subjects felt their parents had pushed them extra hard in school because of their disabled sibling's inability to perform. My family's income had freed me to offer only the care I *wanted* to give (ironically, I would now make a career of it), and David and I knew that our parents would have demanded our best, regardless.

67

At home again with Bob over Christmas break, I gave him the cotton pajamas I'd sewn for him on the machine in my dorm. I also found the opportunity to ask Dad about Baby Jane's condition.

Dad issued a long sigh. "Yeah, hydrocephalus like that is devastating. They don't ordinarily live long, but there are bed after bed of them in Sunland at Fort Myers."

Fort Myers was on the far side of Florida that I'd never seen. Nor had I ever heard of Sunland, but I could see it in my mind's eye—row after row of cribs, each one holding a Baby Jane. *How shocking.* Would I ever see such a place? I was in no hurry.

I was a sophomore the evening I returned to my dorm and found an urgent message to call home. Dad was in the hospital, Mother said, with a myocardial infarction.

In tears I asked, "Shouldn't I come home?"

"No, honey, it looks like he'll be okay. Stay in school."

It was the first of three heart attacks over two decades, but we were lucky; he survived them all. With his first, he stopped smoking and slowed his work pace, cutting his practice by half and assuming the part-time chief-of-staff position at St. Mary's.

I worked five days a week in his office over the summer and dated Hugh MacMillan, the hunky, Princeton football tailback whose family had been Hillcrest neighbors and patients of my father's.

On my twentieth birthday that June, the mean-faced governor of Alabama made headlines by halting the desegregation of the University of Alabama. On the heels of that drama came Dr. Martin Luther King Jr.'s March on Washington, but what grabbed me and shook me to the core was the shocking violence against blacks in the news reports. Even within our all-white enclave of Palm Beach, I'd understood that virtually all blacks lived in poverty and lacked the many privileges my friends and I took for granted, but as sure as my brother was crippled, I suffered my own disability. I had been blind to the injustice and violence that rained down on blacks while we were growing up in the Jim Crow South. Nor had I noticed the indignity within our own home when, as youngsters, we called all our black helpers by their first names—even Herman, the silver-haired gentleman who came each Christmas Eve to help Mother serve our holiday feast.

The current news clips and photographs of blacks who were hosed, beaten, or worse, had me thinking of Julia Hillman, horrified by the thought of her and her loved ones being mistreated like that. I'd never had a black neighbor, classmate, or teacher, never met an educated black person, but even I could see that it was all terribly wrong.

I enrolled in two classes at Manhattan's NYU the summer before my senior year in order to finish Duke a semester early and get on with graduate school. Dad wasn't thrilled about my New York escapade, but he offered a suggestion: "While you're there, check out the Rusk Institute of Rehabilitation Medicine. They handle an incredible array of conditions. You should volunteer there."

It was my first day as a candy striper when I slipped into my red-and-white pinafore in Rusk's first-floor ladies' room and headed for the elevator. Stepping into the vacant car, I noticed that the woman who followed me on was pushing a stroller. Glancing at her child, I realized he had no arms. The doors closed with only the three of us onboard. He cooed and looked around. Eyeing him again, I saw he had no legs. I would *not* let this throw me. Lifting my eyes to the mother, I chirped, "He's so cute." Honest, he was.

Her face froze, eyes on the wall, her lips barely moved. "Better that he hadn't lived."

The door opened and I stepped off, utterly aghast at her words.

My father explained on the phone: A new drug used to combat nausea—Thalidomide—had been prescribed for many expectant mothers, some of whom took it at a critical time when their fetuses' limbs were forming. Apparently, the babies' brains and other organs were unaffected.

I played and read books with another limbless child at Rusk, an adorable three-year-old black girl, who'd been abandoned at birth and spent her life thus far on their pediatric ward. A little ball of fire, she used the tiny flippers where her limbs would have been to scoot along the floor, and boy, she talked a blue streak, charming everyone she met. Her nurses said she was learning to use prosthetic legs and would acquire most self-help skills. Soon she would live with a foster family, perhaps be adopted. Their optimism was contagious—or was I wearing those rose-colored glasses Mother had accused me of wearing?

Hugh was an hour's bus ride away that summer, in Princeton, NJ working in a program for underprivileged boys. Each Wednesday afternoon he came into Manhattan for an evening of fun—as much as five bucks could buy—and on Fridays, I rode the bus to Princeton for the weekend. He dragged me to a gathering of his program's staff, insisting I meet their director, Dr. Preston Wilcox. Dr. Wilcox was a professor of social work from Columbia University, a charismatic, stereotype-busting, black intellectual—and for me, a revelation.

GRADUATE SCHOOL AND MARRIAGE
(1965–1966)

Columbia University Teacher's College was an easy choice for my master's degree in special education. In addition to the New York school's top-notch reputation, Hugh—now my fiancé—was one block up Broadway at Union Theological Seminary. At the end of my first semester at Columbia, we flew home together, a week before our June wedding.

Hugh's mother and mine were old friends and more than happy to be running the show together, allowing Hugh and me a little time for the beach, less than a hundred yards from my parents' house. Hand-in-hand, we strolled up to the inlet, admiring the gin-clear water in this tropical paradise where we'd both grown up, yet knowing our appetites were whetted for more exciting venues.

On Friday, high swaths of clouds swept another perfect Carrera-marble sky, the Atlantic beckoning again, but it was our wedding eve, and the beach out of the question. I was too tied up to go out to the airport to greet Bob and Julia.

"I suppose you want him home for your wedding," Mother had said months before

"*Of course*, Mom!"

When my parents brought them back to the house, the two kept us company in the living room while Hugh and I opened a few gifts—more Gorham and Lenox to add to our embarrassing stash of riches.

I turned to Hugh. "Let's take him for a walk."

"Pretty hot out there. Wanna go up to the beach?"

"His chair won't go on the sand."

"It's okay. I'll carry him."

Julia piped up. "Y'all going in the water, Anne? You want his braces off? I can do it right quick."

I looked to Bob. "What'cha think, kiddo?" A thrilled grin, his arms thrust outward.

"It's a bird! It's a plane..."

He hadn't been to the beach since we were little, so we slipped into suits and grabbed towels while Julia stripped Bob to shorts and a T-shirt.

"Y'all have fun," Julia said. "Don't let the fish bite your toes, Bob!"

"Ahhhhh."

Barelegged in flip-flops, we wheeled Bob up to the little cinder block cabana at the end of our street where we abandoned his chair and carried him across the narrow slip of beach. Spreading towels just short of the gently lapping surf, we tried holding him in a sitting position between us, but he was too excited to bend at the waist, so we sculpted a hole for his boney rump, lined the hole with a towel, and set his butt in. With Hugh's cap and shades, Bob finally looked comfortable—a stylin' surfer dude.

With the breeze, it seemed unwise to take him in the water, so we lolled there on the beach, watching the fishing boats that bobbed beyond the breakers, the tankers that clung to the horizon. Hugh and I rubbed his hands across the warm sand, scooped salty froth, and dribbled it across his feet. Bob's eyes tracked the sandpipers scurrying between us and the water.

I pointed. "Look at the pelicans, Bob!" They were dive-bombing for fish, one by one, grenades exploding the water's surface. We laughed and narrated their falls, "Errrrr—*Boom!*" Hugh and I had seen these things countless times, yet seeing them now, through Bob's eyes, was exquisite pleasure, a rare opportunity to share the beauty and excitement of this special afternoon with the brother I couldn't get enough of.

When it was almost time to head back, we awkwardly maneuvered Bob onto Hugh's shoulders so his legs straddled Hugh's neck and Hugh grasped Bob's forearms to hold him upright.

"Okay, bub?" Hugh asked.

Catching the grin beneath Bob's drooping head, I assured Hugh, "He's okay."

With my ankles wedged into the warm sand, I watched the odd tandem amble down the crescent of the beach: my fragile, helpless brother on the brawny shoulders of the young athlete I would marry. With each step Bob's head bounced loosely, his inert legs dangling like snapped fronds on a storm-whipped palm. My fiancé was at ease with my brother's anomalous frame. He accepted and valued the part of me that was Bob's sister. Awash in happiness, I couldn't imagine marrying him otherwise.

Hugh and I spent our first year of marriage in Oxford, England, where Hugh had a fellowship to continue his theological studies and I found work caring for children in a small mental hospital. Living abroad was an exciting adventure, but Christmas apart from family—without Bob—was pure misery.

The timing of our return to the Big Apple the following September was auspicious. The year before, 1965, Congress had passed Public Law 89-313, allocating $85 million over the next four years to help the fifty states extend educational services to all handicapped children. New York's allotment covered my tuition at Columbia Teacher's College, plus a two-thousand-dollar stipend for living expenses. Hugh reduced his classwork at Union Seminary so he could take a pastoral internship at Sea and Land Presbyterian Church on Henry Street in lower Manhattan. The internship gave us a rent-free apartment in the church parish hall and another two grand to boot—we'd hit the mother lode.

All my life, I'd been steeped in plenty of plenty. Now, the challenge of getting by on next-to-nothing became a point of pride. The sum of our possessions was a queen-size mattress, a meager closet of clothes, and our cache of impractical wedding loot still stashed in my parents' closet in Palm Beach. Like many of our contemporaries, we reveled in a different kind of prosperity: the hectic excitement of the city, the multiethnic character of our as yet ungentrified Lower East Side neighborhood. Two blocks from our apartment, Yiddish-speaking Jews shopped kosher delicatessens; two blocks in the opposite direction, ancient Asian immigrants slurped nests of noodles in below-street-level Chinese restaurants. Every Sunday, black, white, Puerto Rican, and Asian families from the housing projects filled our

75

church sanctuary. And on Friday nights, teenagers of every creed and hue jammed the coffee house Hugh ran in the church basement.

On weekdays, I student taught at United Cerebral Palsy's preschool in Brownsville, Brooklyn—about a forty-five-minute commute south from Manhattan—and three nights a week, I schlepped up to 120th Street via subway for class.

My courses now zeroed in on the topics that most fascinated me, neurological impairments and physical disabilities. One class, taught by Dr. Michael Smith, a practicing neurologist, held me spellbound. Each assigned reading and lecture illuminated my brother's condition. Simply stepping into that classroom made my heart pound.

I relished my new insights about seemingly trivial things, such as Bob's long-standing aversion to furry stuffed animals: individuals with brain damage are prone to confuse inanimate objects with animate ones. I learned why he grew agitated every time I tried to entertain him by playing the piano: perceptual problems, common among this population, can make music sound like a jumble of disparate notes. Alternatively, maybe my playing was *that bad*.

I knew little about reflexes (the automatic movements our bodies make in response to certain cues) or their importance in relation to cerebral palsy. When I had seen Dad and his partner, Dr. O'Hara, tap patients' knees and elbows with plexors, I knew they were checking reflexes, but, until now, I hadn't a clue why.

They were screening for neurological problems. At birth, normal newborns exhibit certain primitive reflexes that subside over ensuing months, but children with neurological problems or cerebral palsy are apt to retain these early reflexes. One such reflex is the Moro or startle reflex. On cue, when something like a loud noise startles the baby, a newborn abruptly throws his head back and extends both arms outward as though reaching for an embrace. *Hmm...*Bob had done that—involuntarily thrown his head back and extended his arms out in front of him—whenever he was startled or excited. *"Up in the sky—look! It's SuperBob!"*

What I had dubbed his "power surge" was actually a pronounced Moro reflex, which he should have outgrown by the time he was five or six months old.

Dr. Smith spoke at length about another primitive reflex, the asymmetrical tonic neck reflex (ATNR). When a normal, full-term newborn's head is turned to one side, his arm on that side (and to a lesser extent that leg) extend outward while the opposite arm bends up like a fencer. Only after this reflex subsides around the age of six or seven months can an infant hold objects up to his face to inspect them, to see them up close, to smell and mouth and taste them. However, children with neurological problems like cerebral palsy often retain this reflex or have an even more pronounced version of it, preventing their close inspection of objects, and blocking these crucial modes of early learning. Another unfortunate but common, long-term effect of this retained reflex is the permanent bending of the spine, known as scoliosis.

I had an "aha" moment. Throughout our childhood, I'd seen Bobby in that ATNR pose, his head locked to one side in what clearly had been an involuntary position since he often gazed in the opposite direction. And his eyes had continually tracked my every move. Now I understood that Bobby's über-attention—what Mother had encouraged me to see as a reflection of his love for me—had actually been the way he had compensated for his inability to hold and manipulate objects

77

on his own. He had learned instead by watching *me* manipulate those objects. I could hardly wait to see him again, and to check his reflexes. Turning the tables, I would learn through him.

Concluding his final lecture on the topic of cerebral palsy, Dr. Smith invited questions.

My hand shot up. "What can you tell us about life expectancy?" Merely a professional curiosity, of course.

"You mean, do they have shortened life spans?"

I nodded, doing my best to feign nonchalance.

He shook his head. "No, not unless there are other complications."

Not the reply I had braced for. Bob's medical condition was clearly sliding downhill. How could he possibly survive decade after decade? What "other complications" might be causing his physical decline?

DAVID'S DISCOVERY (1966)

David met his wife Kathy in 1962 at Duke Hospital where he was a medical student and she a registered nurse. Early in their relationship, they made an amazing discovery: each had a severely disabled sibling. Kathy explained that her identical twin sister, Arleen, had suffered brain injury from the use of high forceps during birth. Arleen could walk, talk, and feed herself, but she had a severe intellectual disability. David confided that his brother Bob had a whopping case of cerebral palsy with seizures, apparently from infantile encephalitis. Although Bob was mentally alert, his eyes were the only part of his body he fully controlled.

Kathy and David married shortly after David's graduation from medical school. Following a two-year residency at Duke, they moved to Rockville, Maryland, where David fulfilled his military obligation during the Vietnam War. He worked as a post doc and a public health officer at the molecular biology lab for the National Institute of Arthritis and Metabolic Disease.

Two of David's friends from high school, Lois Faville and Bill Kelley, had married and moved to Rockville. Bill was also an MD at the U.S. Public Health Service. One evening, while Lois helped Kathy, who was eight months pregnant, put the final touches on dinner, David and Bill talked shop in the living room, drinks in hand.

Bill spoke of his latest project with Jay Seegmiller, chief of human biochemical genetics at NIH's National Institute of Arthritis and Metabolic Disease. "We've found the enzymatic defect associated with a syndrome that Bill Nyhan and Mike Lesch at Johns Hopkins identified a couple of years ago in a small number of young males with severe, spastic cerebral palsy. It's called Lesch-Nyhan syndrome. The missing enzyme is Hypoxanthine-guanine phosphoribosyltransferase, HGPRTase."

David was familiar with the enzyme and its role in purine metabolism because as a medical student he had worked in the lab of a recognized expert in purine metabolism. (Purines are critical components of DNA that are found naturally in food. Metabolism is the process whereby our bodies digest DNA, releasing purines and breaking them down to form urate or uric acid.)

David was intrigued by this claim of a genetic basis for cerebral palsy because cerebral palsy was generally attributed to neurological trauma, inadequate oxygen, or infection (such as Bob's purported encephalitis). He asked Bill for more clinical description.

"Mild to moderate mental retardation, dramatic hyperuricemia, urinary tract infections, uric acid stones, hematuria, and gout." Hyperuricemia referred to an unusually high concentration of uric acid in the blood. Hematuria meant blood in the urine.

David, now rapt, leaned in. Bob had repeatedly experienced urinary tract infections and uric acid stones. He showed no sign of gout, but Mother had suffered pain from gout in her toes for decades.

Bill continued. "Nyhan says the boys tend to be alert and socially interactive, but they have an unusual behavioral pathology—a compulsion to bite their lips and fingers."

Bill's description transported a stunned David back to his childhood. Bobby was crying and pulling his hand toward his face. Mother grabbed his hand and told him, "No! No biting!" Bobby's thumbnail looked as though he'd caught his thumb in a door, when, in fact, the bruises were from biting his own fingers when Mother hadn't been there to stop him. Sometimes he bit so hard he broke the skin and the wound took days to heal. Bobby's biting behavior had been sporadic and relatively mild by comparison to other boys with Lesch-Nyhan syndrome, but it was a clear pattern. Each piece of the puzzle fit.

Three weeks later, David walked into Bill's lab with a test tube of blood. "Hey, Bill. I brought you something. How about assaying HGPRTase in this blood?"

"Where's it from?"

"When you've assayed it, if it's missing HGPRTase, I'll reveal the source."

Bill shrugged and took the anonymous sample. Only three Lesch-Nyhan syndrome diagnoses had ever been confirmed by assays that showed the absence of HGPRTase, but he would run the test and let David know.

When Bill reported the blood sample was, in fact, missing HGPRTase, David was hardly surprised. The blood sample had come from Bob. David had asked Dad to arrange for Bob's physician in Atlanta to draw the sample and send it to him. For more than two decades, Bob's doctors—including our father—had attributed Bob's brain damage and seizures to an encephalitis infection during Bob's

81

first year of life. David now knew better: Bob's condition stemmed not from infection, but from an inherited deficiency of HGPRTase.

Kathy was due to deliver any day now. Although it is typical for adults with disabled siblings to worry that their offspring will be born with the same condition that affected their sibling, David and Kathy's circumstances were doubly worrisome. Kathy knew her sister's condition stemmed from a birth injury and therefore was not inheritable, but the emotions of expectant parents—even those who are medically trained—can outweigh such logical assurances. David now knew that Bob's condition *was* inheritable. Could David, an unaffected male sibling, pass Bob's Lesch-Nyhan syndrome to his own offspring? The answer to this question depended on how the trait was passed on.

Drs. Lesch and Nyhan had studied the syndrome's pattern of inheritance, finding it was X-linked recessive—meaning the faulty gene was located on the X chromosome, as in hemophilia and red-green colorblindness. Carrier mothers passed the faulty gene on, as shown in the diagram on the opposite page. Each male offspring of a carrier mother had a fifty percent chance of being affected and developing the syndrome. Each female offspring of a carrier mother had a fifty percent chance of being a carrier.

Males have only one X chromosome, so if a male inherited the X chromosome with the defective HGPRTase gene from his carrier mother, he would develop the condition. Bob had drawn bad luck, inheriting the defective HGPRTase gene and, consequently, developing the syndrome. David had been spared. Since he hadn't inherited the defective gene, he had no defective gene to pass to his offspring. David and Kathy had no rational basis to be concerned about their offspring having Lesch-Nyhan syndrome.

But did I?

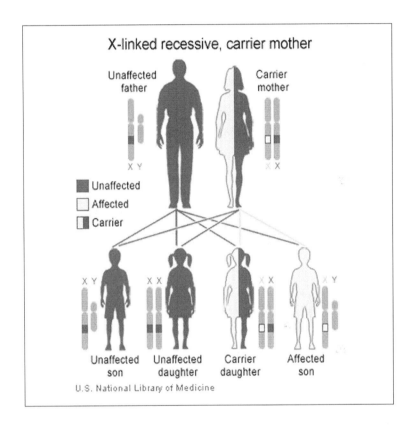

Because females have two X chromosomes, a woman who inherits a faulty HGPRTase gene on one X chromosome (i.e. "a carrier") would have another X chromosome that would be highly likely to have a normal HGPRTase to compensate for the defective one. Consequently, even if a female offspring inherited the faulty X chromosome from her carrier mother, she would not develop the syndrome. However, she would be a carrier and have a fifty percent chance of passing on the faulty X chromosome in each of her pregnancies. The cycle would continue, generation after generation, as long as carrier females produced offspring, unless medical scientists— like David and his friend Bill Kelley—found a way to stop it.

Was I an "unaffected daughter" or a "carrier daughter"? This question set off a succession of events that would lead me down a path I never thought I would take.

When Mother sent Hugh and me tickets to fly home to West Palm the following spring, David scheduled a visit to coincide with ours. Several months before, he had called and asked me to pull twenty hairs from my scalp with root follicles intact, place them in the test tube he would send, and mail it back to him.

"You've got to be kidding!" I wailed. "You're trying to torture me, like you did when we were little?" In fact, I knew the reason for his odd request. He had already collected hair samples and a skin biopsy from Mother that confirmed she was indeed a Lesch-Nyhan carrier. The odds of my being a carrier were fifty-fifty, so he needed hair samples and a skin biopsy from me as well.

During our visit, Dad drove David and me across the bridge to his office where I climbed onto the exam table and eyed the syringe of Novocaine in my brother's hand.

"Which arm?" David asked, a glint in his eye.

"Like I care, you sadist!" I couldn't hold my pout for laughing. "Oh, on the left, I guess—underneath, where it won't show."

With Dad's surgical punch in hand, David confessed. "I've always wanted to cut on you!"

"Don't think I don't know that!"

With Dad crowing at our banter, David got his jollies by

carving a 3-mm hole under my arm. Then he stitched it up, and we headed home for dinner.

Hugh and I drove his parents' VW bug back to New York for our final few months there, stopping in Atlanta on the way. Although the Gatchells were expecting us, Bob was not out front waiting. He was stuck in bed with a pressure sore on his butt.

I had thought only frail, old folks who languished in bad nursing homes suffered from pressure sores. Bob was twenty-two and clearly receiving highly attentive care. His bones, I imagined, had finally concluded they were riding in a substandard vessel and decided to bail.

Prone in bed, Bob reared his head and chest off the mattress to offer a hearty groan of welcome. More emaciated than ever, his adolescence had belatedly kicked in. His baby face had matured, his voice dropped, his hair was a darker shade of brown. And he'd experienced an amazing growth spurt, making him look nearly normal in height, though measuring him would have been a tall order. His scoliosis (the curvature in his spine) was so pronounced he looked practically folded over sideways. He'd been unable to tolerate his braces for a while. As I recall, he had not bitten himself in years, though he was so incapacitated I doubt he could have maneuvered his hands to his face had he tried.

"Hey, lil brother," I said, bussing him. "What's that growing on your chin? Won't Mr. Gatchell loan you his electric razor?" The famous grin. A TV squawked by his bed. "Seen any Dinah Shore specials lately?" Every time he heard Dinah's throaty voice, he would melt into a goony smile, especially if it was "I've Got a Crush on

You." As I teased him about his girlfriend, he fluttered his eyelids in pretended ecstasy. Same old Bob.

He had to stay off his backside until his bedsore healed, but Julia turned him over on a cloud of sheepskin and pillows so I could feed him lunch. It took more than the usual time and coaxing, but she said we did okay. Once his sore healed, he would be able to lie on his back again but only on sheepskin and with frequent repositioning to prevent further skin breakdowns. He would need to sit in a slightly elevated recliner rather than erect in a chair. Mrs. Gatchell said she had ordered a special air mattress with an electric blower to inflate alternate channels, automatically shifting his weight every few minutes.

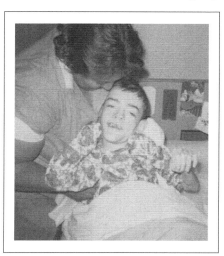

Bob's condition was disconcerting, but at least we knew Julia and the Gatchells would take good care of him. *Thank God for them.*

Before hitting the road, we snapped Julia helping Bob say "cheese."

A month after we'd met in West Palm, David called. "I hate to tell you…" he began.

I assumed he was calling with the biopsy results. "Go ahead, David, lay it on me."

"Unfortunately, the lab had an accident and burned up your biopsy."

"You're kidding!"

"Afraid not." He sounded humbled—not the David I knew—though the accident had occurred in Dr. Seegmiller's lab, not his own.

"You're having way too much fun with this, David. So I have to do it over? Another damn biopsy?"

"Right. You'll need to have your doctor do it this time. I'll mail you a kit with instructions. And, while you're at it, send me another batch of twenty hairs as well. Sorry about the screw-up. Really, I am."

"It's okay, David. I'm just razzing you. I'll make an appointment with my gynecologist."

Two months after my doctor mailed the second biopsy to David, he called again, this time with results: I was *not* a carrier. Welcome news, though I hadn't worried about it, my interest in motherhood still latent.

Mother and Dad called on two separate occasions to report that Bob was in the hospital in Atlanta. He was having difficulty getting his food down and keeping it there—an upper gastrointestinal obstruction, most likely due to his severe scoliosis. I had seen how twisted and folded his torso had become the last time I'd seen him. From what I had gleaned from my study of neurological impairments, I understood that Bob's abnormal reflexes—in particular, his pronounced "fencer" reflex (ATNR) that caused him to bend to one side—were wreaking their predictable havoc.

At the time of his first hospitalization, Mother and Dad were in Chicago at a medical seminar, so David flew to Atlanta to oversee Bob's care. Soon they called again, this time with news that blew me away: the Gatchells had decided that Bob's condition was so fragile they could no longer care for him. When the Atlanta hospital discharged him, an ambulance would transport him directly to St. Mary's in West Palm.

When my parents met Hugh and me at the West Palm Beach airport late in the day, Mother's shell-shocked face told the story. She was depleted, physically and emotionally. Since Bob's arrival ten days before, she'd been camping out at St. Mary's—and not just to keep him company. She could do a better job of getting food and drink down him than some nurse he didn't know.

We dropped Hugh at his parents' house and headed home, Dad at the wheel.

"How's Bob doing now?" I asked.

Dad's reply came in stops, starts, and sighs. "Not as sick as he was. Seems stable for now. Overall, he's gone downhill quite a lot. You know, Anne, he's pretty much like an old man now."

Dad's stark assessment stung. They had called me with updates on his condition, but the reality hadn't sunk in.

"I need to get back to St. Mary's," Mother said, "and give him supper."

"No, you don't," I countered. "I'll feed him. You take the night off."

"Okay, sweetheart. Sure could use the rest. He knows you're coming and is excited about seeing you."

At home, as we headed for the kitchen, Dad handed me his entry card for the doctor's parking lot and turned to Mother. "Want a drink, dear?"

She hesitated, as though thinking it over. "Oh, I guess so."

I smiled to myself, knowing her ambivalence was pretense.

Surely, a nightly Scotch or two was the crutch that helped her wade through this grueling time. As a teen, I had resented her nightly libations. It was easier now to cut her some slack.

As I entered Bob's hospital room, trepidation tempered my excitement about seeing him.

"How ya doing, bub?" A hand on his shoulder, a kiss.

He lay supine—the bedsore now healed—and eyed me. "Ewww," he said, phlegm rattling in his throat.

"Yeah, I've missed you too. I hear you've been in the hospital a lot. Not much fun, huh?"

"Ooooooo. Ahhh."

"David came to see you in the hospital in Atlanta, didn't he?"

"Uhhhh!"

"Was he a big help, now that he's a hotshot doctor?"

"Uhhhh." Bob's vocalizations now resembled groans, rather than the crisp, easily distinguishable *Uhs!* and *Uh-uhs!* he had previously managed. But his eyes, facial expressions and body language—whether stiffened or relaxed—conveyed his feelings.

"I'll bet the nurses here know Daddy. Are they giving you special attention?"

"Awww."

The dinner tray materialized: red Jello and pureed mystery food.

"Here's your supper, Bob. You hungry?" A grimace said "no."

Once upon a time, eating had been a pleasant commune with family and peers—especially when the fare was Bobby's favorite, spaghetti and meatballs from Tony's Italian. Come each and every

Sunday evening, the three of us would ride out Okeechobee Boulevard with Daddy to pick it up. Tony always invited us back to his steaming kitchen where he dipped his giant ladle into the monster pot and extracted a few mini-meatballs for Bobby. "For you, my bambino, I make aspeshal for you."

Back home, Mom would tuck a towel in Bobby's collar and the show began with Bobby channeling the protagonist in his favorite storybook, *George the Greedy Pig*. Mother lifted his shirt to show his full, swollen belly and teased, "Come on, Bobby, you don't want more, do you?" But he insisted, "Uhh!" his grin outlined in sauce, the towel a crimson mess.

Now, eating had become a chore.

Hugh and I slept in the following morning while Mother headed to St. Mary's. I claimed the afternoon shift. Hugh dined with his parents that evening while I had dinner with Mother and Dad on our lanai. "What happens with Bob now?"

"Your dad and I were wondering what you think we should do."

I was stunned. They wanted *my* opinion? After the way they tore him away from me as a child? Of course, I was an adult now, trained in a related field, no less, and they were stumped. "Gosh, I dunno. What are the options?"

"Well," Mother said, "we've checked into a few nursing homes."

"God, no!" It was a knee-jerk response. Dad's comment aside, Bob was no typical old man. All I saw he had in common with seniors was his imploding body.

"I don't suppose you could get help and bring him here?"
It was more a statement of fact than a serious question, and highly
unlikely, I knew. There was nothing like a hospice to help—at least not
in West Palm. Besides, Mother and Dad had never seemed to consider
that kind of life-altering, open-ended commitment as feasible. Years
before, when Dad's own father developed dementia and became
physically combative, Dad had driven him to a state psychiatric
hospital in South Florida where he had him committed. Mother told
me when Dad returned home that evening, he sobbed all night in his
pillow—another painful yet undiscussed decision, harkening back to
their decision to send Bobby off to Atlanta. Another Big Unspoken.

Dad jumped in reply to my question. "No, no. We can't handle
him here. He needs close medical supervision, around-the-clock
nursing care."

I dared not press. "Well, what else?"

Mother sighed. "Well, there's Sunland."

I knew zilch about institutions for people with disabilities.
Even at Teacher's College, I'd never heard of New York's soon-to-be-
infamous Willowbrook State School. I was in England in 1965, when
Senator Robert Kennedy had famously called Willowbrook "a snake
pit." But I remembered back in college when Dad had lamented those
rows and rows of beds holding Baby Janes at Fort Myers' Sunland.

"You mean that place in Fort Myers?"

"No. There are six Sunland facilities. The two in Orlando and
Tallahassee are hospitals for non-ambulatory patients. The one in
Orlando serves our area."

"Well, what do you know about it?"

"We drove up there last week for a look," Mother said.

They'd already checked it out? *Wow.* This train was moving fast. Granted, I hadn't been the one to spend day after day with him at St. Mary's.

"Well, what'd you think?"

Dad measured his words. "It was clean. Orderly. We met with the medical director, a guy named Carter. Quite a knowledgeable fellow, familiar with the type of medical issues Bob has now. They have quite a few patients who are in the same boat as Bob."

"We were impressed with the guy," Mother interjected. "Seems really involved and dedicated." She hesitated, her eyes on her plate. "But we just don't know if it's the right thing to do. What would you think about our putting him there?"

I imagined Sunland similar to St. Mary's Hospital. "Well, it sounds like his medical care is what's most important now. If you think the Sunland doctor's familiar with what Bob needs. To me, a place with other disabled people sounds better than an old folks' home. At least Orlando's closer than Atlanta."

"A three-hour drive from here," Mother said.

"What's the process to have him admitted?"

"We completed some papers while there," Dad said. "Next is an evaluation of his mental capacity."

I scoffed. "An IQ test? How, pray tell, are they gonna do that?" Measuring the IQ of a nonverbal individual was hardly a simple task.

"They'll send someone to St. Mary's to observe him. Soon, they said."

It was a lot to take in. I had naïvely assumed there must be some reasonable solution, but there wasn't. To challenge their stance that they couldn't bring him home would have been tantamount to questioning their love for him, which I knew full well was as deep as my own.

I thought of Ronald, one of my favorite students back in New York, a cute, five-year-old black child with severe cerebral palsy. Ronald's teacher had told me that his parents had him on a waiting list for one of New York's state institutions. Low-income families like Ronald's ran out of options sooner than families like mine. My parents' income and serendipitous friendship with the Lanes had enabled them to keep Bob out of an institution all these years, but in the end, his medical needs forced their hand.

Entering Bob's room at St. Mary's on the day before our return to New York, I spied a stranger by the window, a clipboard in his lap. I greeted my brother and then turned to him. "Who are you?"

"Oh, sorry, I'm Stan Roberts from the Florida Department of Health and Rehabilitative Services, here to observe Mr. Martin."

"I'm his sister. So you're from Sunland?"

"No, but I conduct psychological evaluations for Sunland applicants. If you and Mr. Martin don't mind, I'll stay just a few more minutes."

"Okay by you, Bob?" I asked.

"Ewwwww." If not, he would have grimaced.

We ignored the guy and soon he left. That is how my twenty-two-year-old brother was officially crowned "mentally retarded," making him eligible to join the line for admission to Sunland Hospital in Orlando. I doubt that guy with his clipboard had the slightest grasp of what went on inside my brother's cranium, but it mattered not. The label wasn't the point. Our family needed help and quickly.

Our Sea and Land Church sat at the foot of the Manhattan Bridge where the D-Line ran over to Brooklyn. As a result, our pathetic little kitchen atop the parish hall shuddered and shook during rush hour for at least three minutes out of every ten.

While the trains roared by one evening, I worked on dinner and simultaneously indulged in warm, fuzzy thoughts of Bob. I was a pretty darn good sister to him, I knew, but for some reason I couldn't fathom, my heart kept telling me otherwise. Why did I have this persistent feeling that I'd failed him?

A long-buried memory suddenly bubbled to the surface: Bobby lay facedown on the sidewalk, his trike strapped to his back, Mother working frantically to disentangle him. *Oh God, his bloody face. That terrible knot on his forehead—all of it my fault.*

Leaning on the Formica countertop, I reeled from the guilt and shame of that awful incident, shedding the tears I'd fought to contain nearly two decades before. How I wished I could do right by him now, but he was impossibly far away.

Seeing More of Bob (1967–1969)

By the time I finished my degree at Teacher's College that June, Hugh had decided to trade seminary for law school at the University of Florida, aiming for a career at the nexus of politics and poverty issues. I would be our breadwinner for the next two-and-a-half years. I found a position teaching a special class of EMR (Educable Mentally Retarded) students in a black elementary school in Archer, Florida—a small, rural community outside of Gainesville where "all deliberate speed" was taking its own sweet time.

I had hoped to teach students with more severe disabilities, but at Teacher's College I'd been warned that, outside of major metropolitan areas like New York, classes for severely disabled students were rare. Perhaps this was because nearly two hundred thousand individuals with disabilities resided in our country's public institutions (U.S. DOE 2007). As for those severely disabled children who lived at home with their families, most states, including Florida, were just beginning to gear up to serve them.

Teaching at an all-black school was an appealing prospect, but best of all, Gainesville was only a two-hour drive to Orlando—the closest Bob and I had lived to each other since we were youngsters.

Following Bob's admission to Sunland Hospital at Orlando, Mother had driven up to visit him several times, but Dad accompanied her only once. "He simply can't handle it," she told me over the phone, her own despondency audible. "He literally falls apart."

Now twenty-four, I could see my family's circumstances in a more sympathetic light: The healer had no cure—not even a salve—for his own son; he caved beneath the weight of his impotence. The drive to Orlando was too hard for Mother to undertake alone on a frequent basis. David was in San Francisco, tied to his research and teaching at University of California San Francisco's Medical School, with two young children at home.

I could not bear the thought of Bob feeling abandoned by his family. I could go see him on weekends. In my Episcopalian heart, it felt "meet and right" to assume this rather adult role, though it was less "bounden duty" than the opportunity I had longed for—a chance to see more of him.

Visit 1

Mother and I met in Orlando at Sonny's Bar-B-Q where, over sandwiches, she outlined the protocol. "Call them at this number ahead of time, give them a good half-hour notice. I use the pay phone here before I order. When you arrive, check in at the front desk. The receptionist will notify the staff on his living unit—it's Unit 3A. Take the elevator up to the third floor and wait on the bench in the hallway. When they bring him out, take him down to the first floor. There are visiting rooms down there, or you can take him out to the picnic tables behind the building. When you're ready to leave, take him back up to the third floor and use the house phone to speak with the operator. She'll call the unit staff to retrieve him."

I followed her to Sunland in my car. It was a few blocks off Colonial Drive, insulated from a residential neighborhood by a sprawling lawn and parking lot. Pulling up, I took in the monolithic, four-story, classic government-issue building of white stucco with crank-out windows rimmed in a dull, dark green. A wide bank of steps rose to the second-floor entrance. In the large, stark entry hall, a rotund matron in a tight Toni perm and flowered frock glanced up from her switchboard and asked how she could help us. Sitting across from her was a pale, competent-appearing young man in a wheelchair, evidently a resident. I would see him in this very spot nearly every weekend I visited for the next two years.

We took the elevator up and waited. I was determined not to cry. I hadn't shed a single tear for my brother in the presence of my parents since my seminal visit to the Gatchells, and wasn't going to start now. But when they wheeled him through the metal swinging doors, the sight of him bowled me over. They had practically shaved his head, as though preparing him for brain surgery or to be strapped to the electric chair. On a wheeled recliner, he groaned aloud, his back arched, his head craned back at a ninety-degree angle, his breathing noisy, conveying his excitement about seeing us. When I leaned down to embrace him, I had to turn my face so he and Mother wouldn't see my struggle.

As we descended in the elevator, a tear ran down his cheek. Over the years since, I've tried to convince myself that it was just the harsh fluorescent lights making his eyes water, but then I recall how his lip quivered too, and I lose it.

But with Mother and I chatting him up, he smiled and talked with us. The place was about as personal and inviting as a meat locker. I clung to the hope that someone who tended him—*Please, God, just one kind and perceptive person*—would notice how alert he was, talk with him, and give him a little personal attention.

Visit 5

I was cooling my heels on the hardwood bench when a gaunt, white-haired man in wire-rimmed glasses, lab coat, and scrubs vaulted from the double doors of Bob's living unit. Looking surprised to see me there, he walked over.

"Hello, I'm Dr. Carter. Is someone helping you?" The badge announced he was the medical director. Mother and Dad had been impressed by him.

"I'm waiting for my brother."

"And your brother's name?"

"Robert Martin—he's been here a few months."

"Yes, of course. I remember your parents, and I know who your brother is."

"You do?" I choked with relief. This man was responsible for the care of hundreds of residents (nearly a thousand, I later learned), yet he knew Bob.

"Yes, I've checked on him nearly every day. Seems to be getting along fine, though he does present somewhat of a medical challenge. I've spoken with your parents several times to update them."

The metal doors groaned open. "Ewwwww." Bob's voice had grown as deep as any young man's. A heavyset woman in a white uniform shoved the door with her backside, wheeling him from behind. He lay supine on a blue Naugahyde recliner, tricked out in long pants with a mock Nehru shirt and fake-gold hippie necklace—Mother's touch of humor. At this point, the getup was more grotesque than funny.

I stooped to kiss him. "Hey, bub." Nuzzling his cheek a few extra seconds, I checked my tears—never easy when I first laid eyes on him. "I'm so happy to see you, Bobalinski. I just met your doctor and I like him. Let's take the elevator down and talk."

Visit 17

This time Hugh accompanied me, which I appreciated, not only for his company on the drive, but because he could lift Bob from his recliner to the couch in the visiting room. That way Bob's head and shoulders rested on the cushion in my lap and I could hold him close while we talked face-to-face.

"Bob, do you remember when you and Julia used to fly to West Palm for Christmas?"

"Ewwwwww."

"Did you like flying? Did the stewardess bring you some Coke?"

"Ahhhhhhhhh."

"And remember that summer you and I fished at Hillstream?"

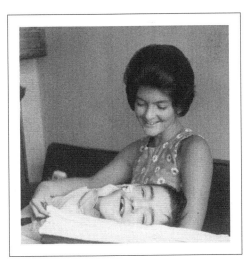

In one of Sunland's visiting rooms. Bob's nasogastric tube is taped to his cheek.

99

It was the only summer when Mother's promise that we could see Bobby in the summertime came true. The second summer after he left for the Gatchells, Mother's friend, Sis Harms, gave us a gift we would never forget. Her family owned Hillstream Farm outside Dahlonega, Georgia, an hour's drive north of Atlanta. "Come on up," Sis told Mother, "and bring Bobby!"

Their farmhouse sat astride a roaring waterfall and rushing stream. Bobby really, really, really wanted to fish that stream. The Harms had cane poles and a manure pile of worms, but David—our family's expert fisherman—was at summer camp, so I agreed to take my brother fishing.

Daddy pushed Bobby's chair through the red-clay mush, secured it on a broad, flat boulder by the water's edge, and left us. I peered at the pink mass writhing at the bottom of our tin can and, over the roar of water pounding rock, I whined and complained. "Ewww, gross, Bobby. You don't expect me to touch them, do you?"

Amused by his sister's revulsion, Bobby about split his sides laughing.

I had observed David and Mother's technique for skewering worms on hooks, but could never stomach doing it myself. "No, Bobby—I can't. I swear I'll throw up!"

Threading the length of that sucker, I gagged. Bobby laughed harder.

Our worm properly impaled, we wrapped our hands around the pole and together lobbed the hook toward the deepest looking spot, raising the line at frequent intervals to check the worm's status. Again and again, the worm was gone. Were the fish nibbling them away, or was the current stripping them from the hook? "Please, Bobby," I pleaded, "don't make me hook another one!"

I suppose the water's roar may have drowned out the sound of Bobby's whooping and my histrionics, but I knew darn well my parents and the Harms were up in the farmhouse cackling about the torture I was going through. Bobby and I had nary a nibble that morning...

"You had the time of your life laughing at me, didn't you, Bob!"

A wide grin. "Ewww."

The treks to Orlando lent a steady rhythm to our life in Archer. I devoted the bulk of my Saturdays to preparing my teaching materials for the following week, Sundays to the trip down and back, sometimes with Hugh, other times on my own. But after driving down there four weekends in a row, I found myself frazzled and exhausted. Too much time on the road, too little time for me and my husband, so I decided to limit my trips to every other weekend and found that a more pleasant, sustainable pace.

Archer Community Elementary had never had a white teacher (though a Jewish woman, near my age and also from New York, arrived the same year I did). My job and our decision to rent in Archer rather than commute from Gainesville earned us rare entrée into Archer's black community. Along with it came the palpable disdain of Archer's relatively small white population.

My students and I began each morning with the Pledge of Allegiance followed by a few songs. The whole class got off on the James Brown tape I brought in, "I'm Black and I'm Proud," but none more than Mae Jean. At seven, she was my youngest student, with legs like cane poles beneath her two-sizes-too-small dress. An ever present smile was the hallmark of her upbeat disposition. Cutting a sassy little strut, she sang her own version of the lyrics: "Say it loud—I'm black and I'm skinny!"

Before Mr. Brown's song rose to the top of the charts, the word "black" had been an ugly epithet these kids slung at each other.

After song time came "show and tell," that classic exercise for promoting polite listening and confident speaking. It proved to be an invaluable window into my students' lives. I discovered they knew things about which I knew almost nothing. They reveled in my ignorance. I was confused about the difference between a chicken and a hen. They howled. I'd never had gopher soup, didn't know that a gopher was a kind of tortoise, thought it was something furry that burrowed underground. I was unsure what time of year tobacco was cut, which month watermelons ripened in the field, or when pecans fell to the ground. I didn't know the words to even the first verse of "Lift Every Voice and Sing." Land sakes! Where was their new teacher from—the moon?

Our principal, Mr. McGhee, occasionally stepped into my classroom and observed for a few minutes, but I enjoyed complete freedom to teach whatever I decided my students needed. No curriculum to follow, no test to teach to. Halfway through the school year, the prim assistant director for Exceptional Student Education, who had interviewed and hired me, came to observe my teaching for a morning and then stayed over lunch to confer.

After going through the cafeteria line together, we found seats at the teachers' table. On her first bite of black-eyed peas, she choked.

"My, this is spicy," she rasped, her eyes watering.

It was hard not to laugh. What did she expect at a black school? Our kitchen served awesome soul food—iron-rich greens and okra, yams, cornbread, fried chicken, even chitlins—every bite of it blackened with pepper. Over at the kids' table, my students heaped on the hot sauce while my guest worked on regaining her composure.

"I see you're focusing on reading and academics," she said. "I'd like to see you place more emphasis on life skills." She meant topics like personal hygiene, homemaking, and accessing community resources like food stamps and welfare. She had taken my students' formal IQ scores to indicate they were incapable of learning to read and write, but I had discovered early on that their scores understated their learning capacity. The literature in my field would have labeled these students as "culturally deprived." Although none currently performed on grade level, all were keen to read and write, and most were progressing. It would take more than poverty to crush these kids, and they did not live in a cultural desert. Their culture just differed, radically, from the culture of my guest and those who designed standardized tests. I filed her advice under "well intended" and kept pushing the three Rs.

Visit 20

When Bob left the Gatchell School, he had lost his second family—Julia and Mr. and Mrs. Gatchell and the peers he'd lived with for more than a decade. While I hoped someone who worked on his living unit here at Sunland would befriend him, I wasn't optimistic. It seemed all he had now were Mother's visits and mine—not much to live for. With a deep sense of loss for him, I did my damnedest to turn back the clock, to transport him back to a time when he had things to savor, things to laugh about. To remind him that once upon a time, he'd actually had a life.

"Bob, remember the musicians who serenaded us at our Sanford Avenue house?"

We had been teenagers that New Year's Eve when our parents went out partying and David and I stayed home with Bob. Julia had bathed him and retreated to her room, but he was still awake upstairs when I heard music wafting from our front yard. In the circular driveway outside our living room stood three black gentlemen in tuxedoes—the trio that often performed at Testa's Restaurant a few blocks away—one with an accordion, the other two with makeshift percussion thingamajigs. Strolling up our street, they were serenading each house with lively renditions of Christmas carols, looking for tips.

I bounded upstairs, yelling, "David! Some guys are out front caroling. Let's get Bob downstairs so he can see."

We rushed him, clad in pajama top and diaper, down to the living room where, to hear better, we opened the window, its ledge mere inches off the floor. David held Bob's right flank and I held the other as he teetered on his toes, the three of us in full view at the window. The ragtag band launched into "I'm Dreaming of a White Christmas" with the palms rustling overhead. We joined their song, Bob contributing in his unique way. "Ewww..."

These gentlemen seemed undismayed by the odd sight of our brother. They were smiling and singing with gusto. Then I noticed they weren't just smiling anymore; they were laughing hard, their eyes aimed at Bob's feet. Bob, too, began to shake with laughter. Glancing down, I saw his diaper around his toes, the family jewels on resplendent display. The three of us crumpled to the floor like dominos, our hysteria severely hindering our efforts to cover Bob up. The minstrels moved on down the street that night without a tip from our house, but we'd given them a kookie flasher story.

"Remember how Mother laughed when we told her, Bob?"

Of course he remembered—I saw those wheels whirring behind his eyes.

Visit 29

I warmed my highly coveted spot in the hallway, having phoned from Sonny's a generous half-hour before I arrived. I must have waited here at least another thirty or forty minutes, so I picked up the house phone and asked the receptionist to call the unit staff again. *For crying out loud, how long can it take them to dress him and wheel him out?*

I thought about marching right through those doors and fetching him myself, but I refrained for a couple of reasons. For starters, the sign on one of the doors thundered "NO ADMITTANCE, Authorized Staff Only." In addition, the people who worked behind those doors controlled how my brother was treated day and night. The last thing he needed was his sister breaking their stupid rules and ticking them off. And frankly, it was a bit unnerving to imagine what I might encounter back there. Did I really want to search bed after bed of deformed people to find my brother? No, I would stick to the protocol—stay put and wait.

Visit 35

Bob's hair had grown way too long and was slicked back with some kind of oil that made it dark and greasy. I hated the look. It reminded me of those greasers back in high school. I imagined one of the black caregivers must have fixed it that way since I knew a lot of blacks pomaded their own hair. Or had someone anointed Bob with holy oil—Unction for the Sick?

"Remember Holy Trinity, Bob?"

"Uhhh!"

"And the times Father Stirling came down to our pew and blessed you?"

I suppose the most generous thing I might have done for him was to give voice to his feelings about the reality he now endured, about how he missed Julia and the Gatchells, to acknowledge how hard it was for him to live apart from those of us who loved him.

But honestly, I wasn't up to the task—not even close, afraid I would drown us both in tears. His and my own. Maybe it was better not to stir his emotions.

Visit 40

With the glorious weather, I tried taking Bob out to the picnic tables—a break from the bleak ambiance of the visiting rooms—but the glare outside seemed to bother him, and the area was rife with gnats. The dadgum things loved the friggin' grease in his hair. They swarmed him. Tired of batting them away, I wheeled him back inside to the monotony of the visiting room and our favorite orange "pleather" couch.

I rubbed his bony shoulders and toothpick arms, and we chatted more.

"Remember how much Julia liked visiting Palm Beach, Bob?"

"Ahhh."

"Remember when you and she walked down to the Kennedy house?"

I was in high school and we'd just moved to Palm Beach's North End when Mother, Dad, and I made our annual trek to the airport to pick up Bob and Julia. The main route back home to our significantly smaller house carried us past the Kennedy estate, a Mediterranean Revival mansion close to the road, behind a bougainvillea-draped wall. The car in front of us poked along at a maddening pace, its occupants gaping at the famous residence. "Rubberneckers" the locals would have called them, but our ever impatient father had his own epithet: "Goddamn tourists!" Driving like a bank robber as usual, he stomped the pedal to the metal and veered around them, yellow lines be damned.

"You know, Julia," said Mother, "that's President Kennedy's house. Some of his family must be in town. The folks behind the rope over there are hoping for a glimpse of them."

"No," Julia said. "Hear that, Bob? The president lives there! You think he's there now?"

"Not sure," said Mother. "Think I saw in the paper he's coming sometime over the holidays."

When I came home the next afternoon, Bob and Julia were nowhere in sight.

"She took him for a walk," Mother said. "They've been gone a while. I expect 'em soon."

Changing to short-shorts, I headed out to the driveway to wash my car, the butter-yellow MG coupe Dad had handed over once I'd mastered the stick shift. I had the hose blasting when I spotted Bob and Julia coming through the sea grapes up on Ocean Boulevard.

Bob's face aimed back at Julia as she pushed him, trotting at a clip, her mouth running per usual.

At the edge of our yard, she cried, "Anne! We got something to tell you!" Reaching our driveway, panting and glistening, she urged, "Tell her, Bob! Tell her!"

He eyed me, then Julia, lifted his chin, and let fly a forceful, "UHHHH!"

"Where've you been?" I laughed. "You didn't go down to the Kennedys', did you?" A twenty-minute trek.

"We saw him!" said Julia, her chest still heaving. "We saw Mr. President! Didn't we, Bob?"

"You walked all the way down there?"

"Sure worth the walk, honey. That big, black automobile pulled up, one police in front, one in back, red lights aflashin'. Mr. President, he climbed out and waved at us 'cross the street, then in through the gate. I can't wait to tell my family—Bobby and me, we saw President Kennedy!"

When she called her family in Atlanta that evening, I heard her bubbling over with news of their sighting. "I'm in Palm Beach, honey. Bobby and me, we're having a wonderful time!"

It was the sharing of memories like this that sustained us.

"Well, time for me to hit the road again, kiddo. I love you so much. Yep, you love me too. See you Sunday after next—I promise."

Visit 45

On a rare midweek visit, I was killing time on the hallway bench when a young woman stepped from the elevator and sashayed through the doors of Bob's living unit, returning minutes later with a young girl in a wheelchair. While they stood in front of me waiting for the elevator, I seized the moment. "Excuse me, do you work back there on the living unit?"

"No, ma'am, I'm a teacher's aide."

"Well, do the teachers or teacher's aides ever work with the adults?"

"We have so many children and our teaching staff's so limited, we don't get around to many adults."

It figured. Mother had wrangled a few hours a week out of the public schools for Bob, but he'd never received his fair share of public education. Now he'd aged out—too old for a teacher's time. It stuck in my craw, big time.

Visit 48

Bob and I rode the elevator with an elderly couple who were wheeling an adult resident—their daughter, I supposed. It was hard to miss the fact that visitors around here were downright scarce. On Sunday afternoons, general hospitals would be swarmed during visiting hours, but Sunland's visiting rooms lay mostly vacant. Bob and I *owned* the place.

If we happened to encounter another visitor, we would nod "hello" and help each other hold the doors for the wheelchairs, but rarely did we introduce ourselves. Introductions seemed superfluous. We were already open books to each other, knowing all too well what the other felt: the resignation that someone else took care of our loved one now, someone who didn't know or care about small things such as how we used to fix their hair; the guilt about not coming more often or staying longer; the grief held in check—until we surrendered our loved one to the white uniforms again, and hurried back down the steps to the parking lot, wiping the errant tears from our cheeks.

Visit 53

Tooling down I-75 South on my way to Orlando, I fiddled with the dial on the radio. Most stations along this route featured country music or "hell-fire" preachers, but I would eventually find some pop I could groove to, crank up the volume, and sing along. If other drivers caught me singing to the windshield, that was their problem, but I tried to draw the line at letting them see me bawl. Truth be told, I spent a fair amount of my driving time ruminating and emoting, my tears triggered and stoked by sappy love songs. This time it was Sinatra crooning Rodgers and Hart's "My Funny Valentine," the lyrics pegging my feelings for Bob: "Your looks are laughable, unphotographable, but you're my favorite work of art. Is your figure less than Greek? Is your mouth a little weak? When you open it to speak, are you smart?"

A decade's worth of unspilled tears breached the dam that day. I could barely see the road ahead. Never again could I hear that song without thinking of Bob and wanting to weep.

Halfway through our two-and-a-half-year law school project, something clicked and I began to pine for a baby. Parenthood didn't exactly jibe with our plans or household budget, but screw it all—I stopped taking the pill.

Month after month, my period kept coming. Hugh and I submitted to every humiliating test my gynecologist could dream up, revealing no cause of infertility. I swore that the next time my doctor told me to "just relax," I would knee him in his privates. After months of disappointment, I began to believe it simply wasn't in the stars for me to get pregnant—at least not now, not as long as Bob needed me. A baby might curtail our visits.

But by the time Hugh started his final semester of law school, every bleeping couple in his graduating class was expecting, except us. "Why don't you two jump on the bandwagon?" his classmates asked.

I hated them. Fortunately, I'd been fascinated as a young girl when my father found two precious newborns for my Aunt Mary Hart to adopt. Doctor placements were legal in Florida, but not in her state of California. Seeing adoption as an appealing solution, we asked my gynecologist to help us. Expecting a lengthy wait, we kept our plans secret, even from our parents. The only one I told was Bob.

Three weeks before Hugh's December graduation, we collected our three-day-old infant at a Gainesville hospital and gleefully sprinted with her in my arms across the parking lot to our car. We'd beaten most of our pregnant friends to the finish line.

Following Hugh's graduation, we packed our baby and everything we owned and drove to West Palm Beach for Christmas, stopping briefly in Orlando. There, in Sunland's third-floor hallway, we placed little seven-pound Sarah on Bob's stretcher, mere inches from his face. What good would my happiness have been if I couldn't share it with him?

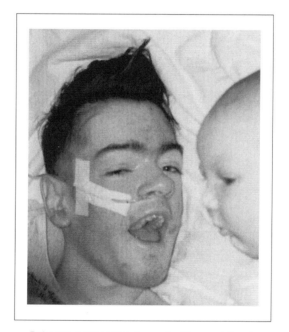

Bob was extraordinarily excited to meet Sarah.

THE DISTANCE BETWEEN US
(JANUARY 1970–FEBRUARY 1972)

Hugh's first job out of law school was in Washington, D.C. where he worked for the Legal Services Office in the U.S. Office of Equal Opportunity. Nixon was president; I was a full-time mom. We flew to West Palm twice that year. Mother and I drove to Orlando both times, but those quick, drive-by visits tore at me. By the time we got back to West Palm, I was doubled over in pain, my stomach in knots.

Back at our apartment in D.C., my angst haunted me.

I crawled in the dark, my hands and knees pressing on a crude, scratchy blanket. Something beneath the blanket kept moving— something hard and long, like the bones of a skeleton. I tried, but couldn't maneuver around them. Nor could I turn back, my mission too important.

Jolted awake, I was sobbing in my own bed, my heart racing.

"What's wrong? Why're you crying?" my husband asked.

"Those bunk beds in the concentration camp—I dreamed I was climbing over the prisoners in there, trying to find Bob."

When we lived in England four years before, Hugh and I had visited the former concentration camp at Dachau, Germany, where we studied photographs of hollow faces peering from tightly stacked bunks. Their emaciated bodies and limbs resembled Bob's.

That November (1970), Hugh's office landed at the center of a political maelstrom. When Donald Rumsfeld, director of OEO, fired the director of OEO Legal Services, Hugh's future employment looked iffy, so he sent out feelers for other positions, including one to work for Florida's Governor-elect Reubin Askew. When that offer came through right before Christmas, we jumped at the chance to return to our home state. Our new home would be in Tallahassee, a five-hour drive from Orlando. Better, but too far for day trips.

Scanning *The Tallahassee Democrat* one morning not long after we moved, I read an article about the staff at a local hospital complaining of low wages and difficult work conditions. They had scheduled a walkout march.

It was January 1971, a time when protest marches were hardly rare. The American Civil Rights Movement had staged marches and sit-ins all over the South throughout the '60s, but for me this march was extraordinary. The hospital in the spotlight was Tallahassee's Sunland Hospital. The protesters were counterparts of the staff who cared for Bob at Sunland Hospital in Orlando—the people who literally held the quality of his life in their hands. Their work was crucially important; they should be paid decent wages and treated well. I thought of Julia and all she had done for our family.

On the appointed morning, I packed up Sarah and her paraphernalia and drove to Saint Mary's Primitive Baptist Church where a small crowd of African-Americans, mostly women, had begun to gather out front. The man in the clerical collar was Reverend Gooden, pastor of the modest brick church and the group's spokesperson. We would walk the mile-and-a-half to Tallahassee Memorial Hospital (a few workers from that hospital had joined the protest) and then the final mile to Sunland.

Our procession wound beneath a canopy of ancient live oaks draped with Spanish moss that hung like icicles overhead. The day was warm and sunny. With motorcycle cops blocking traffic, I felt perfectly safe pushing Sarah in her stroller down the center of the street, chanting and singing with the others. We stopped for some speechifying in front of Tallahassee Memorial, the march proceeding more slowly than I had anticipated. Worried that Sarah might have a meltdown, I decided to skip the final leg of the march and take her home. It was the best I could do with a one-year-old in tow.

The following evening Hugh arrived home from work wearing an amused grin. "You'll never guess what happened this morning."

"Oh yeah? What?"

"We had a meeting with Sheriff Hamlin and some officials from the Department of Health and Rehabilitative Services—the department that oversees the six Sunland facilities. The sheriff had a videotape of yesterday's march. So we're watching the tape and someone pipes up, 'Who's that white woman with the baby stroller?'"

"Oh jeez—you didn't, did you?"

He laughed. "Why not? Told 'em it was my rabble-rouser wife—that you have a brother at Orlando Sunland and a special ed degree."

"They have a problem with me being there?"

"Sheriff didn't look too pleased, but the Division of Retardation's

Jack McAllister—the guy over the six Sunland facilities—said he'd like to meet you."

"Why?"

"Believe it or not, I think he's interested in hiring you. Asked for your number."

His secretary called a few days later, saying, "Bring your resume."

Mr. McAllister wasn't the droll bureaucrat I had expected, but a personable guy, tall and trim, with an amazing radio-announcer voice, and fired up about the job he'd held for only a few months. He told me that he, too, had been drawn to the field of disabilities because of a family member. One of his twin girls was a special child. Prior to assuming this position, he'd served as executive director of Florida's Association for Retarded Citizens, the group of parents who banded together in the late fifties and sixties to advocate for services for their children. He aimed to build a statewide network of training programs and other support services to help families keep their disabled children at home, and to enable developmentally disabled adults to live as independently as possible within their communities. He spoke of the nationwide deinstitutionalization movement, a movement based on reform strategies developed by President Kennedy's Panel on Mental Retardation. Kennedy had urged Congress to pass legislation to reduce the population in state institutions.

Everyone knew that John and Bobby Kennedy's sister Kathleen had an intellectual disability. In 1965, Bobby Kennedy had toured New York's Willowbrook State School with a camera crew and pronounced it a "snake pit." Like my own brother, Kathleen Kennedy had clearly lit a fire in her siblings' bellies, fires that drove them to do something to improve the lives of people with disabilities.

I was impressed—even inspired—by McAllister's passion. His vision sounded a lot like the Reverend King's vision of a just and inclusive society.

"I see you have a Master's in special ed. Would you be interested in working with us?"

"I don't think I could handle a full-time job right now. I guess you saw I have a toddler."

He laughed. "The one in the stroller! Well, how many hours do you think you'd be able to work?"

"Half-time maybe, but I'd need to find child care first."

He nodded, leaning back in his chair. "What are your interests?"

"Persons with cerebral palsy. And minorities, especially African-Americans."

He thought for a few seconds, stroking his chin. "How about looking into how well our division serves our state's minorities? Could you pull together a report on that topic?"

"I think I'd like to tackle it."

"You can work whatever schedule suits you. My secretary will put you in touch with our staff. They'll help you gather the information you need."

The perfect part-time work had just dropped into my lap. All I had done was take a walk with some folks I felt indebted to. Even as he lay in Sunland, Bob was still busy charming my life.

My report, submitted several months later, indicated that Florida's meager array of day training programs for developmentally disabled individuals served proportionally fewer blacks and Hispanics, yet these minorities were significantly overrepresented among the residents of the six Sunland institutions. Their want of community-based services likely contributed to their higher rate of institutionalization.

McAllister brought me on board part-time as one of his assistants. I did my share of schlepping for him, but he also set me to work on drafting a procedural manual for the Sunlands with the goal of moving each institution toward compliance with current professional best practices, even though they would require additional funding to comply fully. I also routed his mail, much of it from vocal parents and advocates who objected to his "cockeyed plans" to phase out the Sunland institutions. What if, some worried, after the Sunlands were shuttered, the state fell on hard times and cut funding for the community supports that families had grown to depend on, pulling the rug out from under them?

From my front-row seat, I saw how my boss addressed the employee unrest at Tallahassee Sunland. The superintendent soon resigned, and, following a nationwide search, McAllister filled the position with a talented, affable gentleman from Kentucky named Dr. Charles Kimber, a psychologist and, incidentally, a black man. The staff discontent evaporated.

I shared a small office with June, a friendly lady about twenty years my senior, who wore her Clairol-blond curls piled atop her head, Lucille Ball style. She coordinated admissions to all six Sunland facilities. When I got around to mentioning that I had a brother in Orlando Sunland, she asked if I'd like her to pull his admission file.

"Okay, I guess I'm curious," I said. "His name's Robert Martin."

She pulled it from the drawer and began flipping through the tabs. "Yes, I remember him now. The application was urgent—we gave it a five, our highest priority. Let's see, he was medically fragile, in St. Mary's Hospital in West Palm. Here's a letter supporting his application from a Dr. O'Hara. It says Robert's father is in extreme distress, has already had two myocardial infarctions. Dr. O'Hara is afraid if Robert isn't admitted soon, his father will have another."

As June read aloud, I recalled my parents' faces across the dining room table, worried sick about Bob, anxious about their daughter's reaction to the sad, limited options for Bob's care.

"We're wondering," they'd said, "what you think we should do."

Sunland, a ray of hope; Sunland, their worst nightmare coming true.

I spoke with Mother and Dad by phone at least weekly now. My motherhood status had pushed the reset button for our relationship, especially with Mother. Besides, what better audience for sharing the cute things our little Sarah was saying and doing? A toddler now, her speech was developing well ahead of expectations. Two decades of yakking at my nonverbal brother had made it seem perfectly natural to bombard her with nonstop chatter, and it was paying off.

But this evening, our topic was Bob. Around the time of his Sunland admission, he'd received a nasogastric tube (a narrow plastic tube inserted through one of his nostrils and down the back of his throat into his stomach in order to provide liquid nourishment). Whether it was inserted before or after his admission, I don't recall, but the tube is visible in every photograph I have of him at Sunland.

I had stupidly assumed the tube would be removed when his eating problem was resolved.

"Dr. Carter suggests Bob would be more comfortable," Mother said, "if his nasogastric tube were replaced by a permanent gastrostomy."

"What's a gastrostomy?"

"A feeding tube," Dad explained, "inserted directly into the stomach through a surgical hole in the abdomen."

I had seen Bob occasionally gag on his nasal tube, and his nose looked a little swollen, but the thought of an incision in his stomach made me wince. "Will it hurt?"

"No, they'll anesthetize him. As with any surgery, he'll have some discomfort afterward, but they'll medicate him for pain, and it should heal quickly."

"Is it risky?"

"No, a simple procedure, with a local anesthetic. I do think he'll find it less irritating."

"When will it happen?"

"Within the next couple of weeks. We'll keep you posted."

I hung up with a miserable, sinking feeling. Dr. Carter had recommended the gastrostomy to make Bob more comfortable. Dad had talked it over with David, and both found it reasonable because, over time, the nasal tube risked eroding his esophagus. But for me, the fact this tube would be permanent underscored a fact I hadn't faced up to: Bob's eating problem wasn't going to go away.

Over the years, there had been few things Bob could actually do with his family, but he could sit at the table and eat with us, at times making us hoot at his gluttony. Food was love. Meals were togetherness. But no more.

I was in West Palm visiting Mother and Dad when I ran into Janie Tedder (mother of my childhood playmate Rita) at a party. Delighted to see each other again, we stepped aside to a quiet corner, our conversation quickly transcending small talk.

"How's Bobby?" she asked. "I've wanted to ask your mom when I saw her, but was unsure…"

"To tell the truth, Janie, not so great. You know, he's fed through a stomach tube now."

Her eyes brimmed. "Is he still alert?"

"He knows us for sure, but it's hard to tell how much more he's taking in. Dad can't handle seeing him there at Sunland."

She swallowed hard. "I hate saying this, honey, but I wonder if it wouldn't be better if he—if they just let him go."

On the verge of tears myself, I told her, "I hear what you're saying, Janie," hugged her, and stepped away.

Busy at home and at work, I usually managed to keep my angst under wraps, but each time I went to see Bob I struggled. His smiles were fleeting now, eye contact was minimal, physical condition the usual wretched. His breathing was noisy, his entire body cable tight. Was he agitated or in pain? I couldn't tell. I felt terrible about not seeing him more often, yet when I was there, I felt pressed to get back home. On my way back from one of those visits, I entertained a radical solution: I might hire an ambulance to bring him to Tallahassee, and he could live with us. But I knew Mother and Dad would be appalled. They

121

would forbid Dr. Carter to release him, out of concern for me. Besides, he was so fragile, he might die en route. And even if he survived the trip, how could I arrange the extensive medical and nursing care that he needed?

Lying awake late at night, I stewed about Bob's circumstances, feeling helpless and wishing I could do something. At my nadir, I wondered if, the next time I went to see him, I should press a pillow to his face and hold it there. But who the hell was I to think I knew what was best for him? Where was that Merciful Father I knew as a child?

Hugh and I attended a keg party at our friends' lakefront home one balmy December evening. The usual state government crowd was there—staff from the Governor's office and legislature and a few bureaucrats like me—milling around the screen porch, enjoying how the postcard-tacky sunset over the lake was turning the water into marmalade.

I stood by the door to the living room, conversing with Janet Reno, a tall, redheaded attorney and state senator's aide. She and Hugh worked together, but the two of us hardly knew each other. When I told her I worked at the Division of Retardation, she visibly stiffened.

The previous week, *The Orlando Sentinel* had run banner headlines about Orlando Sunland and the extraordinary number of patients there who were fed through tubes—gastrostomy tubes in particular. Critics alleged that the tube feedings were medically unnecessary and only for staff convenience.

"Have you ever been to Orlando Sunland?" she asked. "Have you seen that place?"

She looked agitated. She towered over me. I offered a cautious "yes."

She went on. "Did you know that nearly a third of all gastrostomies in all U.S. institutions are right there in that one Sunland?"

"Not until I read it in *The Sentinel.*" I should have left it there, but couldn't. "Well, you know, Janet, some of those patients need to be fed by tube." One in particular, I knew.

My assertion triggered an astonishing, red-faced tirade. "You don't know what you're talking about! Those feeding tubes are for the sake of convenience. That doctor's malicious or incompetent—or *both*!"

In the midst of her rant, I heard myself scream back. "That's not true! You don't know what *you're* talking about!" By this point I was sobbing, but so was she. "My brother's there, and he's riding one of those goddamn tubes. If it weren't for that tube and Dr. Carter, he'd be dead now!"

Over my own diatribe, my head spinning, I heard, "A goddamn concentration camp!"

I spun on my heels, elbowing Hugh on my way out. "I'm leaving now!"

Waiting for him in the car, I struggled to catch my breath, floored by the depth of my own rage.

It seemed that Bob's problems and our country's had converged. While he lay helpless in an institution at the center of a rampant controversy, having received the exact surgical intervention that critics claimed was medically and ethically wrong, dramatic developments in other states were raising the public's awareness about our country's neglect and mistreatment of our mentally retarded and otherwise disabled citizens. Approximately two weeks before my clash with Janet that December 1971, The *Staten Island Advance* published a series of articles detailing the overcrowded and deplorable conditions in New York's Willowbrook State School, America's largest institution for persons with disabilities. In early January of 1972, Geraldo Rivera's television exposé would further inflame the public outrage about the conditions at Willowbrook, and soon similar revelations about other state institutions would come to light. Bob's circumstances—in spite of Mother and Dad's best efforts and extensive expenditure of funds to avoid institutionalizing him—offered evidence of just how deep and pervasive our country's problem had become.

The Orlando Sunland controversy continued to play out in *The Orlando Sentinel* through January 1972 with a couple of state legislators jumping into the fray. When a physician-legislator, Dr. Richard Hodes, toured Orlando Sunland with Dr. Carter, the paper recounted their brutally frank conversation:

In the cases of tube-fed patients, 'We're speaking of beings that have no intelligent life...' (Dr. Hodes) said. He noted the procedure—gastrostomy operation—is keeping alive patients that in similar institutions in other states might have been permitted to die. 'What we have here (at Sunland) is not a case of dehumanization but a unique humane service—one which I question whether the state can afford.'

Dr. Carter took vigorous issue with the implications of the national report that the operation might have been used to make patient feeding easier for hospital staff members. 'The tubes are only inserted after a patient has been proved incapable of eating normally, starts losing weight and would clearly die without the operation.

'And every one of these patients we attempt to spoon feed every day in hopes of getting them to eat normally.

'We do everything we can to keep them alive. I'm not the one to come into a ward, stand up and say, *This child shall die,*' said Dr. Carter. (Stone 1972)

Dr. Hode's reported comments enraged me. How the hell did he know my brother lacked "intelligent life"? Maybe Bob would be better off dead—I had struggled with that very question—but hell would freeze over before our family let some damn politician make that decision.

Feeling compelled to do something, I wrote an angry letter to Dr. Hodes. Aware that he could have me fired at the snap of his finger, I signed it, "Robert Martin, Unit 3A, Orlando Sunland." While I'm not particularly proud of what I wrote, the satisfaction I drew from it was awesome.

My boss Jack McAllister quickly appointed a blue ribbon panel of national experts from the President's Panel on Mental Retardation and three pediatricians from the State Pediatrics Association to examine the high rate of gastrostomies and other criticisms of Orlando Sunland. I had traveled with him to assist in an investigation of resident abuse at another Sunland, so he asked me if I was interested in traveling to Orlando to support the panel again.

"No thanks," I told him. "Too close to home."

The expert panel completed its investigation on February 14, issuing a preliminary report two days later (Bavar 1972). It cleared Dr. Carter and his medical staff of any wrongdoing, but also decried the facility's overcrowded and depressing conditions as well as the fact that it was operated on a medical model rather than a rehabilitative one (Lawrence 1972b).

While the panel compiled its official final report and the Florida Legislature scrambled to pass necessary additional funding that March (Lawrence 1972c), a class-action lawsuit was filed on behalf of the residents of Willowbrook State School's against the State of New York.

The Willowbrook class action would lead to significant reforms, including the gradual downsizing of that institution. Similar class actions would follow in other states, including Florida. Gradually, over the next two decades, these suits would force the downsizing and eventual closure of most—but not all—large institutions for developmentally disabled persons in the U.S., including Willowbrook. The resulting new national policies would emphasize services to help families of disabled individuals along with the provision of smaller, more home-like residences within each disabled person's own community.

But for Bob, these reforms would come too late.

THE CIRCLE OF LIFE (1972)

Mother called late in the day on March 4. Dr. Carter had just called her to report that Bob's condition had worsened since she'd driven up to see Bob the previous week. They had moved him to Sunland's Critical Care Unit.

"Dr. Carter thinks he won't live much longer," she said. "He's resting comfortably, but if you want to see him again, you need to go soon."

He breathed quietly—so serene and relaxed—beneath his oxygen mask. In our green-curtained cocoon, I held his limp, white hand, and we talked. Well, I did all the talking—couldn't help myself. Forever, it had been how we communed. We revisited the warm days and nights of our childhood and spoke of the people we both loved. His eyes never opened; only his chest moved.

Exhausted from my nonstop soliloquy, I spent the night with Mother's friend Sis Harms and returned to his bedside the next morning, knowing I had to get back to Tallahassee that evening. When we'd adopted Sarah two years before, I'd wondered if I was thwarting some divine plan to delay my motherhood as long as Bob needed me, but I had swallowed hard and forged ahead. Now, here I was, wedged between wanting desperately to watch over him at the end of his life, and knowing my daughter needed me at home. We had one more day together, so we talked more. I talked as though my words might keep him alive. The nurse stationed outside our cocoon pulled back the curtain. "You know, dear, he's very sick—you need to be quieter with him."

She was right. I should let him be. In the taxi on my way to the airport, I consoled myself with a plan to return the next week.

On my third night home, I listened to my husband's lullabies as he put Sarah to sleep, then buried myself in his arms. When the phone woke us in our darkened bedroom, Hugh stumbled down the hall for it. Groping in the dark for my nightgown, I heard, "Yes…yes, my wife and I appreciate your calling, Dr. Carter. I'm sorry, too."

"No! NO!" I screamed. "I wanted one more time." Streaking out the back door in my wisp of a gown, I crouched in the grass, hugging my knees, and reeled in deep panic. In my head, I begged him not to go, not to leave me behind. How could I go on without him? In spite of Dr. Carter's unequivocal warning of Bob's impending death, in spite of the unconscious state I'd seen him in at Sunland, I was caught unprepared.

Finally locking onto a bright star above the pines, I found him there, waiting for me. Feeling his presence, I found my calm.

Mother waited until morning to call. We spoke of logistics, then she had a question: "What do you think we should do with his body— burial or cremation?"

"Well, Mom, he was last in line when the guy upstairs handed out bodies, but he ain't stuck in that piece of crap no more. I say burn it!" I shouldn't have vented—not to her—but somehow it moved me forward.

March 1972

Dear Mrs. Martin,

I so, so sorry Bobby passed. When Mrs. Gatchell told me I cry. Mrs. Martin, Bobby love his family more than anything. You and Doctor Martin and Anne and David so good to him. I seen it with my own eyes. I seen how all you family love him.

Mrs. Martin, I know Bobby in heaven now. He find peace in Jesus arms.

Love in Jesus name,
Julia Hillman

After sharing Julia's letter with me, Mother saved it until her death many years later. Then it was mine to treasure and keep, though I still couldn't read it without crying. When I finally began my research for this memoir, I pulled out the letter with my old photos, knowing I would include it word-for-word, and promptly lost it. But, in fact, it wasn't lost, because over the decades, I had memorized every word of it.

Slouched in lawn chairs on a warm May afternoon, my girlfriend and I supervised our two-year-olds' sandbox play while delving deep into girl talk. "Come to think of it," I mused, "I can't recall the last time I had my period. It's been at least a couple of months."

"Better get a pregnancy test, Anne."

"Me, pregnant? That'll be the day!"

I soon deposited the obligatory urine sample at my doctor's office and hardly thought about it. The phone call followed a few days later: "Mrs. MacMillan, we're calling about your pregnancy test. It's positive."

"You're kidding!"

"No, ma'am. Congratulations!"

"Can't be a mistake?"

"The test is reliable, ma'am. You'll need an appointment to come in."

I laughed. I cried. I dialed Hugh at work. "Guess what!"

Our due date was December 8. It took a while for me to connect the dots: December 8 was exactly nine months, to the day, after Bob's death. Mere coincidence? Perhaps, but how could I *not* see this pregnancy as a final, parting gift?

Hugh Robert arrived two days late, on December 10, via an unplanned cesarean section. We called him Hugh Bob, aware that it sounded like something from *The Waltons*: *"Good night, Mom!" "Good night, Hugh Bob!"*

Determined to breastfeed, I had studied *The Womanly Art of Breastfeeding*, but our newborn did not latch on well at the hospital, and no one there seemed to give a hoot about breastfeeding, least of all our pediatrician. The C-section had knocked me flat. A week later, I was exhausted, yet couldn't sleep. Our three-year-old was needy. Our newborn cried a lot. Was he getting enough breast milk? I wasn't sure.

Mother flew up to see her new grandson and help with Sarah. Her assessment came right away. "This baby's dehydrated. You've got to give him formula—or at least a bottle of water."

It flew in the face of all I'd read about breastfeeding. I resisted.

She pulled out all the stops. "If you don't, he could end up like your brother."

Hugh's eyes met mine. "Joanna," he said, "if you keep talking like that, I'll have to put you back on the plane."

She called Dad after dinner. I heard her say, "I swear, Dave, he's so dehydrated the skin on his arms just hangs." She held the phone out to me. "Here, talk to your father."

He pressed, but gently, for once in his life. "I know you want to breastfeed, Anne, and that's good, but it's simply not true that you can't give him a bottle and the breast as well. Let your mother give him formula tonight while you get a good night's sleep, then take him to your pediatrician in the morning to be weighed." So I relented.

In the morning, as we prepared to leave for the pediatrician's office, the doorbell rang. On our front stoop stood my father, a foxy grin on his face. Never had I seen him undertake a single spontaneous act, certainly not chuck a day of work to be with his family. His way, I knew, of saying those three little words I had never heard from him.

When my parents departed the following morning, Hugh and I felt more confident that we had our little family under control, unaware of the next drama about to take the stage.

Less than forty-eight hours after we had taken our son to his office, our pediatrician called. "How're you getting along, Mrs. MacMillan?"

I knew pediatricians. Pediatricians did not ordinarily initiate calls to patients. *Hmm...* What was he up to?

Meandering around to the purpose of his call, he said that because I'd had a brother with Lesch-Nyhan (which I had reported early in my pregnancy), I should take Hugh Bob back to the hospital right away for a blood test.

"But," I sputtered, "my biopsy was negative."

"Yes, this is just an extra precaution to make sure he's unaffected."

He neglected to mention that he had received a call from David (now professor of medicine and biochemistry at UC San Francisco) inquiring about Hugh Bob's uric acid level. Nor was I aware that hospitals routinely drew blood samples from newborns and tested their uric acid levels. An abnormally high uric acid level was a possible indication of Lesch-Nyhan syndrome.

When our pediatrician told David that Hugh Bob's uric acid level was significantly elevated, David had given him an earful.

"That's way too high. You should know that. You need to arrange a follow-up immediately to see if it's receded to normal."

So I carried our ten-day-old baby back to the hospital and allowed a lab tech to dig around in his arm while he screamed bloody murder. "I'm so sorry," she said again and again, "but his veins are so tiny."

Forty-eight hours later, Mother called. "Hugh Bob's uric acid level is within normal range now. He doesn't have Lesch-Nyhan."

"We knew that, Mom. Don't you remember? My biopsy said I wasn't a carrier." Was she losing her marbles?

"I know, but David was afraid your biopsy was wrong since Hugh Bob's uric acid level was sky-high at birth."

"Well, no one said a word to me." I was piqued.

"Didn't want to alarm you unnecessarily, dear, but David and your father have been worried to death that Hugh Bob had your brother's problem."

Our son was two weeks old on Christmas Eve. I was too overwhelmed to acknowledge the holiday—forget stuffing a turkey. While Hugh entertained Sarah, I sprawled on the couch, immobilized. Postpartum blues? Or the first Christmas after losing Bob? Either or both, I couldn't stop crying.

A CONFLUENCE OF NOS (1973)

I received a prescription for birth control pills at my six-week checkup, had it filled at Eckerd Drugs (I'm unsure how promptly), and downed the pills nightly. By February, I was back at work, feeling great, and proud to be managing—with help from our babysitter—my part-time job and two little ones at home.

The scare about Hugh Bob's uric acid level spurred David to send me another biopsy kit. "The procedure's more refined now," he explained, "the results more definitive."

Following David's instructions, our pediatrician extracted the biopsy beside my tiny scars from the previous two and mailed it to David. The results would take a month or more, but who cared? We were sure now that Hugh Bob was fine, and I certainly had no intention of getting pregnant again. My cup runnethed over with the two I had, thank you.

David eventually called with the results. "You're definitely a carrier, Anne. Before you get pregnant again, we need to talk."

The possibility that we might want another child seemed remote, but I figured if we did, I would need to have amniocentesis. I knew next to nothing about the procedure, certainly didn't know anyone who had had one. The scenario seemed far-fetched; I was cavalier.

It was spring when Mother sent me an article about Lesch-Nyhan syndrome from one of David's medical journals, *Hospital Practice*, published a month after Bob's death. The author was Jay Seegmiller, whose laboratory had mistakenly torched my first biopsy. Dr. Seegmiller described Lesch-Nyhan syndrome's signature self-injurious behaviors with the effects depicted in disturbing photographs of the boys' mutilated fingers and lips—far worse than what Bob had exhibited. Other clinical features included severe cerebral palsy with abnormal posture and movements, difficulty speaking or no speech, mild to moderate mental retardation, small stature, and late onset of puberty. In a capsule—Bob. And like him, the boys described were remarkably alert and gregarious. The article addressed the boys' shortened lifespans:

> How long these children live depends to a great extent upon the medical care available to them. The oldest patient we have encountered with the fully expressed syndrome is about 25 years old. Since both of his parents are physicians, he has had an unusual degree of medical attention. (Seegmiller 1972)

I speculated that Bob, who died at twenty-seven, was that oldest patient, albeit the second physician in our family was David, of course—not Mother (hard as she tried). At the point where the article delved into such incomprehensible biochemistry that my head hurt, I stopped reading, inadvertently missing a final, prescient paragraph:

> Prenatal diagnosis…makes possible a preventive program involving selective abortion of proved affected fetuses. The amniocentesis is performed by an obstetrician experienced in the procedure at 16 to 18 weeks of gestation, and the culturing and assay of the amniotic cells require an additional three to four weeks. (Seegmiller 1972)

In May, I noticed a small amount of breakthrough bleeding midway between menstrual periods, so I phoned my gynecologist.

"Any chance you're pregnant?"

"No." I hadn't missed a single pill. *How can I be pregnant?*

"Try doubling the pills," he said. "Take two a day instead of one. Let me know if the bleeding doesn't stop. When's your next appointment?"

"About three weeks from now."

Doubling the pills worked. No need to call him back.

At my appointment, I lay on the exam table, waiting. My gynecologist swooped in, shadowed by his nurse, inserted the speculum, and in a New York minute announced, "Mrs. MacMillan, you are clearly pregnant. I'd say you're at fourteen weeks."

"*Ohmagod* NO*!*" In a panic, my mind raced aloud. "My baby's just seven months old. I've been popping two birth control pills every night for weeks—and I'm a carrier for Lesch-Nyhan. This cannot be!"

He stood over me, his eyes narrowed. "Amniocentesis could indicate whether the fetus is positive for Lesch-Nyhan, but the results would take at least three weeks. At eighteen weeks, you'll be too far along to end the pregnancy. If you decide to abort, your options are limited. You just had a C-section—it's too dangerous for you to go through labor. At this point, the only safe procedure would be a hysterectomy. Time's short. I suggest you go home and talk this over with your husband. I'll need your decision within forty-eight hours."

In fact, the pregnancy was *not* too far along for amniocentesis. Had I studied Dr. Seegmiller's article on Lesch-Nyhan then as carefully as I did decades later, I would have known that the prescribed window for the procedure was actually sixteen to eighteen weeks of gestation. The culturing and assay of the amniotic cells would require, as my doctor indicated, an additional three weeks. By the time we received the test results, I'd have been nineteen to twenty-one weeks along.

In February 1972, a year and a half before, the Florida Supreme Court had thrown out Florida's 104-year-old abortion law prohibiting induced abortions beyond four-and-a-half months (eighteen weeks), except when necessary to save the mother's life, finding the law unconstitutionally "vague, indefinite, and uncertain." With Florida's 104-year old law invalidated, common law applied. Common law prohibited aborting a "quick fetus" (commonly eighteen to twenty weeks or beyond) on penalty of a five-hundred-dollar fine, a year in jail, or both (Lawrence 1972a).

But in January 1973—six months before our crisis arose—the U.S. Supreme Court's ruling in *Roe v. Wade* had invalidated all state laws limiting women's access to abortions during the first trimester, as well as any state law limiting such access during the second trimester, except when the restrictions were for the purpose of protecting the health of the pregnant woman. This meant that Florida's common law eighteen-week limitation on abortion was also unconstitutional.

Nevertheless, my doctor remained wary of crossing the eighteen-week deadline, precluding the test that could have ascertained whether or not the fetus I carried was affected by Lesch-Nyhan syndrome.

A compliant patient, I took my doctor at his word, drove home in a panic, and ran to the phone. "Hugh, I'm pregnant. It's complicated. We have to make a decision right away—come home *now*!"

We had tried to get pregnant for so long that we had never entertained the idea of an unplanned pregnancy. We spent the afternoon mulling over our dilemma, though I confess I saw it more as *my* dilemma than *ours*. Hugh Bob was awfully young for us to have another baby on the way. Being a good mother to Sarah and him was my highest priority, but I also wanted—fiercely—to keep working. I'd lucked into a terrific job with flexible hours and excellent child care, but could imagine no way to juggle another baby and keep working in this or any other meaningful job.

And way back in the wrinkles of my cortex lurked the Lesch-Nyhan threat, supporting what my heart already told me was the right decision. Justifying it. Cementing it. The stars seemed aligned, except for the hysterectomy requirement. Neither Hugh nor I felt ready to slam the door on all future pregnancies.

Sprawled on the couch and encircled by wads of Kleenex, I sopped up the tears. Hunched over beside me, head in hands, sat my grim-faced, former seminarian husband. He suddenly looked up, as if *The Lord Himself* had just called his name. "It'll be okay. I'll cut back at work so I can help you more."

"Who're you kidding? You know damn well you can't cut your hours and keep your job. It's not your career at stake here—it's *mine*." His full-time income quadrupled my part-time earnings. While I appreciated his earning power, the upshot was that my career had become hostage to his. "Let's call David."

David picked up on the second ring. "Hi, Anne, what's up?"

"I'm pregnant again, David, and don't want to be. I just came from my OB. He says I'm in my fourteenth week and can't go through labor because of my C-section. The only way to end the pregnancy is a hysterectomy. Don't want the hysterectomy either. We have forty-eight hours to decide. You know another option to end this pregnancy?"

"Let me check with a colleague in obstetrics. I'll call you right back."

Within the hour he called. "I spoke with my colleague. There's a procedure for inducing abortion, called prostaglandin. It would be safe for you because it wouldn't require you to go through true labor. Jerry says if you fly out tomorrow, he'll schedule you for the procedure the following morning. If you decide to come, I'll pick you up at the airport. You'll stay with Kathy and me."

"Thank you, David. I'll get back with you about my flight."

I had full confidence in David and knew Hugh did too. He'd heard our conversation and knew I intended to have the abortion at David's hospital, avoiding the hysterectomy. He capitulated without further discussion, knowing it was *my* life—not his—that would be radically impacted by another baby—especially one with Lesch-Nyhan. The only remaining question was whether he would accompany me, but the practical plan was for him to stay and care for our little ones. The next morning I boarded the plane alone.

In my brother's sedan, we pulled from his driveway and wended our way downhill. The street uncurled at Mill Valley's center, its shops and cafes still dark. A stretch of red lights, then we geared up to Highway 101 South as I settled into the hug of my soft, leather cradle, lulled by the hiss of tires on wet asphalt.

David sipped from his mug. "Feeling all right?"

"I'm fine."

Beyond a brief tunnel, mist turned to fog. Traffic pushed on, taillights fading in and out of sight. I caught split-second glances of the orange rails and cables in strobe-like flickers. No sight of the towers above, the bay below, the city ahead. Still, I sensed the magic of the Golden Gate.

We threaded the leafy corridor across Golden Gate Park. When scrub-clad walkers flecked the sidewalk, we turned under the sign, *Staff Parking—University of California San Francisco Medical Center*. From the garage, I followed David down the stairwell, through a labyrinth of halls until we faced the entrance for General Admissions. "They're expecting you," he said, "but first you have some paperwork to do. I need to get to my office now, but they'll point you in the right direction. I'll come find you shortly."

He took off down the hall; I dug for my insurance card.

The clerk checked me in and directed me to the elevator for the OB/GYN unit where I approached the nurse behind the counter, handing over my papers. She led me to a small exam room and gave me her spiel about donning the gown. Then, "Dr. Goldstein will be in to see you shortly."

I changed and climbed onto the exam table. Resting against the elevated head of the bed, I sighed. The crisis of my past forty-eight hours was winding down. *God,* I was lucky. I remembered a film from junior high: the frightened teenage girl in a dark alley; the scowling woman who answered her knock and insisted on the cash up front; the man in black who inflicted horrendous pain; the park bench where she spent her final hours, bleeding and alone.

A slight knock, the door swung in.

"Good morning, Anne. I'm Jerry Goldstein." David's colleague was roughly his age—mid-thirties. Owlish glasses, a quick smile. He got right down to business. "I need to examine you briefly, so I'm going to raise your knees now." He slipped on latex gloves. "Try to relax."

I blew the short breaths I had learned in Lamaze class while he confirmed I was indeed pregnant, nearly fifteen weeks along. Removing his gloves, he came to my side.

"So, I understand you had a brother with Lesch-Nyhan syndrome?"

"Yes." My throat tightened, my eyes began to sting. "I did."

"And David tells me your biopsy indicated you're a Lesch-Nyhan carrier."

"Right. The latest one confirmed it."

"And you have an infant son who's unaffected?"

"Yes. He's seven months now and fine." The thought of him brought a smile.

"So then, your decision to terminate this pregnancy must be a clear one?"

I swallowed hard, my eyes piercing the wall.

"Not exactly." It came as a whisper, reflexively honest. I hoped he hadn't heard.

He had and pressed on, his tone softer now. "But surely you wouldn't choose to visit such a devastating condition on another child, since we have the means to prevent it."

My eyes lowered to my cotton gown.

"I know this is the right decision." My voice was thick, my core trembling. "But the truth is…I have mixed feelings." With the back of my wrist, I swiped the tear that hung from my chin.

For the past two days, I'd thought of nothing but the crisis this pregnancy presented, focused on the implausibility of trying to work with three little ones at home. Now I faced the specter of my brother's affliction head-on.

As an adolescent, I had railed against Mother's dark pessimism concerning Bob's future. Then I watched his condition and circumstances deteriorate relentlessly, year after year. All I could do was put one foot in front of the other and go on with my life, as our parents insisted that David and I do.

What happened to Bob still haunted me. At night, I searched for him in my dreams, and in the unforgiving glare of daylight, memories of his devastation lunged at me out of nowhere, making me gasp. In my mother's unguarded face, I saw evidence of the unstoppable force that had ravaged her youngest child. No, I would never want another child to face the fate that awaited Bob. Armed with rare knowledge and David's help, I would stop this predator in its tracks.

But my heart entertained a notion that countered my resolve—a notion that flew in the face of reason. I envisioned having my own son with Lesch-Nyhan, a bright-eyed little boy who would "*eww*" and "*aww*" and flash his sweet smile, lighting up my life the way Bob had.

Through such a son, I might have recovered a tiny piece of the brother I lost. By ending this pregnancy, I foreclosed that possibility.

Grieving for my brother, I reached for the consent form and signed.

A nurse brought a tray of supplies and inserted an IV port into the back of my hand. Dr. Goldstein explained: "We'll give you Demerol to help with the pain, though I think you'll find it only mildly uncomfortable, similar to menstrual cramps. I'll insert a needle into your abdomen and the amniotic sac, drawing fluid to ensure the needle is in the correct position. The injection will stop the fetal heart and cause your uterus to contract. The contractions, though mild, will help to expel the fetus."

His hands palpated my abdomen, the eight-inch midline scar below my navel reminding me of the welcomed birth of Hugh Bob. Anticipating the prick, I clenched the sides of the mattress, clamped my eyes shut. Though painless, I held my breath, fearing the slightest move might hurt.

When I drew for air, my chest wouldn't expand. Reaching for the doctor, I mouthed, "I can't breathe."

His eyes lifted. "Stat!"

I heard the loudspeaker echo his call, felt something slip over my face. When my eyes reopened, I breathed easily again, beneath an oxygen mask. A swarm of white coats. The closest, on my right, was David—the first time I'd seen him in his doctor's coat. He leaned in, my hand in his, and smiled. "I'm sorry, but you're all right now." While I rested, he mused quietly, "It's uncanny how things go awry when an MD's family is involved."

He stayed until his colleague returned, then left us. Through the cloud of Demerol, I felt the head of my bed rise until I overlooked the doctor's hands pressing my abdomen. A swish from my vagina.

My eyes were transfixed on the pad between my thighs: within a dark stain lay a tiny, curled form, the lifeless shape an exact replica of the drawings I'd studied when pregnant with Hugh Bob. I was awed by its minute, intricate perfection. Gloved hands glided into sight, folded the pad over on its contents, and took it away.

I slept.

Awake again, I imagined David in his white coat, somewhere in this sprawling medical complex. He would examine the fetus to determine the gender. A male would have a fifty-fifty chance of having the Lesch-Nyhan gene, a female, the same fifty-fifty chance of carrying the defective gene. Only a biopsy would confirm either. The results would take several weeks. Plenty of time to ask about it—later.

An orderly wheeled me to a different room where I dozed intermittently, glimpsing the fading afternoon through the window by my bed. A nurse helped me dress, then David drove us back to Mill Valley.

Kathy and I were chatting in the kitchen when David held the phone out to me. "Anne, it's Mom and Dad for you." I'd not spoken with them since our crisis arose, but David had called them earlier in the day to fill them in.

Mother's voice was weak. "Oh, Anne, I'm so sorry."

"It's okay, Mom. I'm fine now." It was true. I was.

"Well, your father and I feel terrible that this happened to you."

"No, Mom…please…don't let this upset you."

She was sobbing, each word a struggle. "But…it's all my fault."

"Mom, stop! It's *not* your fault. Why would you say that?"

"Because…it was my gene. It came from me. I'm so sorry."

Oh, God. Like many parents of disabled children, she felt responsible for Bob's condition. I knew this, but was too absorbed in my own drama to realize she would shoulder the blame for this.

"Mom, listen to me. I made this decision because Hugh Bob's so young and because I want to keep working. Even if I weren't a carrier, I would've made the same decision."

Was this true? Honestly, I wasn't sure.

"Anyway, Mom, you can't control your genes any more than I can control mine. Please don't think that way."

She was so distraught, I doubted she'd heard a word I said. I would call her again after I got home.

Back in Tallahassee, Hugh waited at the airport gate, Hugh Bob on his hip, Sarah scaling his leg. Clutching the trio as though returning from Mars, I smeared my tears and nose on my husband's shirt.

For days, my hormones ruled me. I had an overwhelming urge to hold my little ones close, nuzzle their warmth, inhale their fragrance. Still, without missing a beat, I returned to my usual routine, working half-time and taking care of my family.

Over the weeks that followed, I experienced none of the proverbial post-abortion depression—no crying, no second guessing the decision, no tearful discussions with Hugh or my girlfriends, no morose thoughts about the child I might have given birth to. No, what I felt was a nearly euphoric sense of relief, convinced that the possibility of a child's suffering had been averted, and that I had escaped the life-long psychological burden I'd seen my mother bear due to Bob's devastating decline. I had faced what I perceived as a terrible threat and followed a fierce instinct to protect not only my young family, but myself.

I had the babes down for the night and Mother on the phone. We'd spoken numerous times in the two months since my return from San Francisco, cautiously tiptoeing around the topic of my abortion. This evening, with Mother seeming more comfortable about it, we broached the subject head-on. "Maybe it had Lesch-Nyhan," I offered, "maybe it didn't. It doesn't matter now."

Her quiet reply astonished me. "No, it was male, and it had Lesch-Nyhan."

What? Had she really said what I just heard? Where had this come from? David? I could imagine him thinking Mother needed to believe a child with Lesch-Nyhan had been prevented. He might have insinuated...I could call him and ask, or let it be.

By default, I did the latter.

SUNLAND REVISITED (1974–1979)

Orare est laborare, laborare est orare.
(To pray is to work, to work is to pray.)
–Benedictine Order motto

I recorded my initials and the time (6:44 a.m.) on the clipboard that hung on the metal swinging doors and pushed through. Though barely dawn on a Saturday, the chorus was tuning up. Rudi, Ray, and George greeted the day from their beds at the far end of the unit—shrieking, whooping, and bleating. It was a familiar air they were singing, one that made me want to chime in.

"Anne!" called Lucy, giggling aloud from her bed.

"Good morning, Lucy-boosie. Are you ready to get up?"

She giggled more. "Yes."

For the next two hours, I worked at the girls' end of the unit, alongside two middle-aged ladies, Mrs. Jowers and Mrs. Jones. We dressed the children in outfits laid out by the night shift, then transferred them to their wheelchairs, helping each other lift the heaviest. At eight o'clock sharp, the kitchen staff shoved two stainless steel food carts through the swinging doors, the carts' aroma vaguely nauseating.

The children were seated and waiting at long folding tables, a tableau reminiscent of da Vinci's *Last Supper*. Many had special diets, their plates labeled with their names. Some fed themselves; the rest we fed two or three at a time, chatting with them and each other.

I had other responsibilities, but, on the weekends, we often limped along at half-staff, so supervisors like me had to pitch in. That particular Saturday, four of us shared the Sisyphean task of keeping fifty-five developmentally disabled children fed and happy, clean and dry. To cope with the latter task and the odor of ordure, I'd mastered the art of mouth breathing as I wiped little behind after not-so-little behind. The trajectory of my career, a path I deliberately chose, often made me laugh. I was a long way from Palm Beach now—Cinderella, in reverse.

Tallahassee Sunland Hospital, circa 1974

I had first seen the inside of Tallahassee Sunland Hospital two-and-a-half years after Bob's death, eighteen months after my trip to San Francisco. I walked the ground-floor corridor with Denny Reid, the boyish-looking behavioral psychologist who interviewed me the week before and later phoned to offer me the position, at ten-grand less than my salary at the state Division of Retardation.

Pay cut or not, I wanted the job.

"You'll be assigned to Unit 5A, with our highest functioning children. If you come in Thursday morning, I'll introduce you to the folks you'll be working with."

At the end of the corridor, we hung a left and passed a pair of elevators as one rattled open, loosing unworldy shrieks and groans. Two hippie types in jeans waded waist deep in a jungle of wheelchairs and waving limbs.

"We'll take the stairs," Denny said. "With only two elevators, we give priority to staff transporting residents."

We emerged on the fifth floor in a windowless, linoleum-tiled hall. At opposite ends stood two pairs of swinging doors, identical to the ones I had stared at twice a month for two years, waiting for my brother. Waiting while they'd powdered him, exchanged his hospital gown for clothes, and slicked back his hair with that friggin' oil. Those doors at Bob's Sunland bore an intimidating sign that screamed "NO ADMITTANCE!" *These* bore only the clipboard my guide was scribbling on. My heart in my throat, I wondered if I could handle what I was about to see. How tough had it been for Bob behind the doors of his Sunland? *Oh God, don't let me cry, not here, not now.* Drawing a deep, cleansing breath, I followed Denny in.

"This is one of our two units for children," he said.

My eyes scanned the cavernous space, fifty yards long. A sea of white metal cribs lined up like cars in a busy mall parking lot. Unfettered sunlight poured in from an endless wall of crank-out windows. Fluorescent lights and pipes wove a geometric maze beneath the fourteen-foot ceiling. The floors were polished to an aseptic gloss, the walls painted two-toned industrial beige. Two televisions squawked, one tuned to a soap, the other to a game show.

What a dreadful place for children! The mother in me was struck by its sterility—how it lacked the color, clutter, and chaos of childhood. The seamstress in me missed the softness and pattern of fabric. The teacher in me was stunned by the paucity of toys, books, and other objects to see and touch. Not that I'd expected to see a Gatchell School.

By now, I had finally seen the images of Willowbrook State School and similar institutions in Blatt and Kaplan's 1965 photographic essay, *Christmas in Purgatory*, where naked, forlorn children lay on cold, barren floors. What I saw here only vaguely resembled those images. These children wore typical attire and perched in wheelchairs or lay across blue Naugahyde floor mats. Some had heads or facial features that weren't standard-issue shapes or sizes. One child, like Baby Jane at the Gatchell school, had severe hydrocephalus. A few wore helmets to protect them from falls or from beating themselves about their heads, common behavior in environments devoid of positive stimulation. I spotted a lot of children with cerebral palsy. Some wailed or shrieked, most were silent.

"Thirty resident life assistants, called RLAs, work on this unit in three eight-hour shifts," Denny said. "The RLAs on the morning and afternoon shifts are each assigned to a group of eight to twelve children—we call them 'families.' Each RLA bathes, dresses, feeds, and teaches self-help skills to the children in their family group. Their primary supervisor is the unit director. As assistant unit director, you'll be second-in-charge."

These same RLAs must have been the staff whose walkout march I'd joined three years ago, though I didn't recognize anyone. All but one were African-American women, most middle-aged or beyond, attired in street clothes rather than uniforms. I was half their average age and a novice at supervision. The only person I'd supervised had been a teacher's aide, but my two years of living and teaching in Archer had prepared me in one important way: Having witnessed firsthand the strength and determination of Archer's hardworking women of color, I relished the prospect of working with this crew.

"Your main task is to help the RLAs teach these children self-help skills. After you get your feet on the ground, we'll talk about the training programs you'll be setting up."

Denny approached the closest of the children, greeting each one by name. A darling girl with ebony skin and a hundred-watt smile reared back in her wheelchair, her feet climbing the air like a staircase. "Denny!"

"Hi, Lucy!" He squatted and took her hand. "You're dressed so pretty today. Have you been to PT?"

Her head flung back as she managed with obvious effort to say, "She comin'… for me now!" *Oh, the spark in those eyes!*

Denny stooped face-to-face with an appealing, auburn-haired boy, whose pale skin looked nearly translucent. Myron used the word-board on his wheelchair armrests to reply to Denny's questions, pointing to "yes," "no," or another of the thirty-plus words, one of which was "Grandma." Denny told me his grandmother lived nearby and came at least weekly, right onto the living unit where she helped feed him. *Food was love; mealtime was togetherness.* Families were allowed to visit their member's units anytime, Denny said, though it was rare for them to remain so involved.

Some of the children seemed in a deep fog, yet I was astounded to see so many attentive little faces, watching and listening, soaking up everything within sight and earshot. These were children, who, by any standard, had no business being shuttered away in an institution. I wagered that most of them would *not* have been here had the severity of their physical disabilities and the lack of public school programs not made it impossible for their families to cope.

I asked, "Do some of the school-age residents attend public school?"

"Yes, a school bus takes Myron and six others to Everhart School's full-day program."

"So, seven in all? Out of how many?"

"About a hundred and twenty."

"But you have your own teachers on staff?" I'd sought one of those teaching positions, but none was vacant.

"Not enough to meet the need. Our highest functioning children may get an hour or two with a teacher several times a week, but most don't get that much. You'll coordinate the small team of teachers and therapists who work with the kids on this unit."

Right about now I was thinking, *And they're going to **pay** me to work here?*

Over that first year at Tallahassee Sunland, I honed new skills in behavioral techniques, and I stitched gingham aprons for the RLAs to wear while training their children. My aprons—with pockets for positive reinforcements like M&M's and Froot Loops—were a big hit with our ladies. In large and impersonal settings like this, the staff lapped up the smallest signs that their efforts were appreciated.

I heard rumors that a few of our long-haired, hippy types occasionally showed up for work stoned. As for me, I got my high from just walking in the door. In fact, it seemed my whole life was a run-up to being there—beginning with my muse Bob. At times, I heard his voice *ewwing* and *ahhing* down the hall. I saw him each time a child stiffened with excitement or struggled to convey what he wanted—that same unveiled physicality of emotion, that pure glee derived from the simplest of things.

The staff on our unit were handpicked to work with the children, and most seemed to enjoy them, especially children like Lucy and Myron, who exuded a contagious *joie de vivre*. I saw the RLAs bring in clothes from their own children and grandchildren; they even purchased barrettes and ribbons for the girls' hair out of their own pockets. On those days when we were fully staffed and the work pace slowed—the mouths all fed, medications given, diapers changed, BM's charted, children bathed, and bed linens changed—the ladies found time to sit and plait their charges' hair or clip their nails. It pleased me no end to see them lock eyes with a child and issue soft mother-speak. Of course, Sunland had some rotten eggs—staff who left residents in soiled diapers or stole televisions—but they were few.

When I met Venice, a redheaded, crew-cut version of Bob who resided on one of our adult units, he seemed the veritable answer to my prayers. He suffered the same damned combination of mental acuity and total physical incapacitation Bob had, although Venice replied to questions by flexing his knees: once for yes, twice for no. Everyone on staff could see there was a lot going on behind his eyes and were drawn to him. They would chat and interact with him the way I hoped and prayed the staff at Sunland in Orlando had interacted with Bob. Their responses affirmed my faith in the essential goodness of most human beings.

On the other hand, I couldn't help but observe how the daily machinations of even this relatively enlightened institution systematically deprived our residents—especially the adults—of the most basic pleasures in life: their preferences about how and with whom they wanted to live; their privacy and personal possessions; even their pride in themselves. Seeing this made me regret my quiescence at Bob's Sunland. How I wished I'd known how to advocate for my brother and insisted on being allowed behind those swinging doors. Even as I write, I still work on forgiving my younger self.

These regrets fueled my determination to contribute something significant at Tallahassee Sunland. Beyond my assigned responsibilities, I hatched another project, inspired by the Gatchells' beautiful school and one of my favorite Doris Day movies, *Please Don't Eat the Daisies!*

With our institution slated to close over the next decade, the state legislature refused to fund any renovations. But Carole, one of my big-hearted friends, offered to invite her Junior League pals to a coffee so we could solicit their help to make Unit 5A's environment more cheerful and stimulating. Thanks to their generous checks, Unit 5A went *Technicolor*. We covered the cribs and beds with colorful printed sheets, and papered the walls in cute juvenile patterns or painted them in just the right coordinated colors. We covered the dining tables with bright, homey oilcloths, and bought a collection of shiny, new toys. Best of all, our unit's new look seemed to inspire our RLAs. When

Denny and his assistant conducted their rounds of our unit, they found every RLA in her gingham apron, training her assigned children.

Sunland was so important to me that I seized a few opportunities to share it with my own children. On weekends when we were critically short-staffed and off-duty supervisors were called in to help feed the over five hundred residents, I sometimes took Sarah and Hugh Bob with me. Hugh Bob, nearly four, would hop on our unit's Big Wheel trike and rocket up and down the corridor at breakneck speed. Sarah, going on six, was more reluctant. "Sunland doesn't smell very nice," she said, "and some of those kids get on my nerves!" Later, I noticed she'd taped a sheet of paper to her bedroom door and would sign her name as she came in and out. *Monkey see, monkey do.*

That year I took them to Sunland's Easter sunrise service, not your typical Sunday school. Before dawn, we helped a crew of staff and volunteers wheel a hundred blanketed residents—many with contorted torsos and faces kin to Picasso's abstract portraits—out to a verdant rise on Sunland's grounds. There, at morning's first light, our music therapists strummed guitars and led us in song, "Jesus Christ is risen today…"

With the familiar lump swelling in my throat, I could sing no more, but I heard Bob's voice carry the refrain: "*Ahhh-lleluia.*"

I would ordinarily end my narrative here, with my young family and fulfilling work soothing my grief for Bob, but he was no ordinary brother, and there remained a terrible injustice calling for a superhero's intervention. So fast-forward with me another three years to 1979.

I was still at Tallahassee Sunland, but my role had changed. Shortly after we spruced up Unit 5A, Superintendent Kimber had pulled me aside. "I think I have just the right job for you, Anne. Get me your application for program director—if you're interested."

Interested? I would have killed for that position. The program director oversaw Sunland's teachers and therapists, who breezed through the unit doors six days a week and whisked certain lucky residents off to activities that made their lives worth living. This was the *fun* part of Sunland.

The program director also served as Sunland's liaison to the local public school system. Someone was still paving my path. Who could it be? Why, it was SuperBob, of course!

Now that I was an administrator, I was no longer due to work before 8 a.m., but this morning I arrived early. Passing my ground-floor office, I headed directly for the stairwell. Adrenaline stoked, I bounded up to the fifth floor, initialed the clipboard on the doors of my former workplace—Unit 5A—and leaned through.

Mrs. Jowers was helping a trio of girls—ages seven, ten, and twelve—feed themselves breakfast. The girls' barrettes and hair ribbons matched their crisp, new dresses. Nearby, Mrs. Jones patiently fed Carina, a brown-eyed, curly-mopped teenager with intelligent eyes and a whopping case of CP and scoliosis, much like Bob's. I could recall the day three years before when Carina's first menses began, and yet, like the other girls, Carina had never received more than a few hours a week of a teacher's time.

From this day forward, these girls and every single child on this unit would receive a full, six-hour-a-day educational program designed to meet their unique needs.

Like proud mothers, the RLAs at the far end of the unit had their boys well scrubbed, smelling sweet, and dressed in their finest.

The boys' hairdos—no matter kinky, curly, or straight—all had the oily sheen of showroom Cadillacs. I vowed to hold my tongue.

At nine o'clock on the dot, a dozen public school teachers—vivacious, eager young ladies, most fresh-out-of-college, all certified to teach Exceptional Student Education and oozing endless hope—waltzed through the doors with their teacher's aides to collect their new students.

The RLAs turned and stared, hands on hips, sugar-bowl style, offering stiff but polite "good mornings."

Sensing the excitement, Carina and a few of her peers shrieked and reached for the smiling faces of the teachers they'd been introduced to the previous week. Others gazed at the ceiling or floor, oblivious to the special significance of this day, but they too, were wheeled or led down the hall through two sets of swinging doors to their brand-new public school classrooms in a lavishly renovated space.

Until one year ago, the new classroom space—half the length of a football field—had served as home to fifty adults. In an initial step towards closing Tallahassee Sunland, those residents had been transferred to smaller group-living residences.

Our arrangement to house public school classes within the Sunland hospital facility was a negotiated compromise with our county school system. The federal Education of All Handicapped Children Act, enacted four years prior, was still in its initial transition stage, so Florida did not yet require its public schools to serve the hundreds of school-aged residents of the six Sunland Centers. This arrangement failed to comply with the "least restrictive environment" mandated by the federal act, but how long should Sunland's children have to wait? SuperBob was losing patience.

Mrs. Jowers, Mrs. Jones, and I grinned at each other, shaking our heads at the scene. Mrs. Jones dabbed an eye with her gingham apron, then turned and stepped away.

Mrs. Jowers muttered, "Never thought I'd see the day!"

I enjoyed a special bond with these wonderful ladies. It would have been all right, I mused, had they been the ones to care for Bob at his Sunland. I envisioned him with us now, in his chair, rod-stiff with excitement, head thrown back, arms straight out like Superman soaring through the sky. Beside him, his beloved Julia. Together, they hooted, hollered, and waved, drawing a turbocharged kick out of our wheelchair parade.

EPILOGUE

While composing this memoir in 2011, I tracked down Dr. Nyhan who, along with Dr. Michael Lesch (now deceased), first identified Lesch-Nyhan syndrome in 1964. Dr. Nyhan was still conducting research at the University of California in San Diego. He read my manuscript, liked it, and offered to study a sample of my blood with current DNA sequencing techniques in order to identify my family's specific genetic mutation. It sounded like an interesting addition to my memoir.

On March 1, 2012, five months after I submitted my blood sample to Dr. Nyhan's laboratory, I received the following e-mail message:

> Dear Anne,
>
> Sorry it took us so long, but we wanted to be right; so we kept checking.
>
> We could not find a mutation in the coding region of your HPRT DNA. The PhD who does this is quite good at heterozygote (carrier) detection. He likes to eyeball for two bases in one place, as well as the usual statistics.

Without mutational analysis on your brother, we are struck with the probability that you are normal. Of hundreds of patients and families that we have studied, there are a few in whom no mutation was found in the proband patient (the initial family member identified), despite positive enzyme analysis. So this is a possibility; we talked about possible mutations as a regulatory gene, but no one has found one for HPRT. As I have said before, heterozygote detection back when Seegmiller was doing it was notoriously inaccurate.

I can only half imagine how all this makes you feel. My condolences. It might be therapeutic to put this in your book.

Best regards,
William L. Nyhan

I was stunned, but not totally surprised. The years had taught me that even the best of MDs, including those in my own family, were as fallible as the rest of us. Apparently, so were some of their tests.

When I shared Dr. Nyhan's results with David, he explained:

As I recall the comments/results from Jay Seegmiller, the results of your first biopsy showed only normal cells (positive for HGPRT); the second showed only abnormal cells (negative for HGPRT)—about which he was embarrassed that such had been missed the first time.

Normal cells take up hypoxanthine (Hx) and HGPRT traps it inside the cell, leading to the accumulation of Hx inside the cell. LN cells will take up Hx but without HGPRT they cannot trap and accumulate the Hx inside the cell. The HGPRT assay is to feed cells radioactively tagged Hx, and then after some fixed period of time measure Hx accumulation inside the cells.

What likely happened is that the positive result, i.e. uptake of Hx, is real and highly unlikely to be a "false positive" result. The only potential error could be that there were some negative uptake cells that were missed at that time. The second time the assay was done, there was no uptake by any cells observed. "False negatives" in these types of assays are much more likely than false positive uptakes. Thus, Jay's second sets were false negatives; the first were correct—and that is consistent with the sequencing data that Bill Nyhan's lab conducted. The latter are highly reliable.

Convinced that Dr. Nyhan's result was correct, I stewed on what I had learned. Should I have been appalled about the chaos and misinformation that surrounded my decision to abort my pregnancy? Should I have felt embarrassed about my own naiveté and the questions I neglected to ask so long ago?

Picking up Stuart Firestein's *Ignorance: How It Drives Science,* I was reminded that in medical science, as in all science, progress often evolves from uncertainty and chaos. "It is a mistake to bob around in a circle of facts," Firestein claims, "instead of riding the wave to the great expanse outside the circle." (Firestein 2011)

I realized for the first time that David and his colleagues had been riding that wave as they worked in a new branch of science known as genetic medicine. It was 1966 when he and his friend, Bill Kelley, serendipitously uncovered the genetic cause of Bob's condition and David began collecting biopsies from our family. That was the year that Victor McKusick, "the father of genetic medicine," published the first authoritative compendium of human genes and genetic phenotypes, *The Mendelian Inheritance in Man*. In 1973, when I flew in panic to San Francisco, genetic counselors were a rare breed; the earliest programs to train the profession had just begun to produce their first graduates.

My odyssey as a Lesch-Nyhan carrier had been a dizzying roller-coaster ride, but I felt neither anger nor embarrassment, recognizing that David and his contemporaries had been among the earliest gene doctors, doing the best they could—with the limited information available—to help our family avert another tragedy.

Four days after receiving Dr. Nyhan's message, I composed the following message and hit "send."

Dear Dr. Nyhan,

Thank you for your concern. Yes, the results were a surprise, not only to me, but to David. However, when deciding to accept your offer to retest with the most current technology, I understood it might yield different results. I would not have risked pursuing the truth had I not felt sure I could handle it. Had I been pining for another (third) baby back in 1973, the revelation would be considerably more difficult to accept, but as you know from my manuscript, this was not the case.

I believe that, had I not ended that pregnancy, I would have missed the opportunity to process my grief over losing Bob through my work with the residents of Sunland Hospital, many of whom were so like him. Nor would I have adopted another child in 1983, our spectacular son, Martin, whom we plucked from a foster home at the age of five months.

When deciding to write my memoir, I assumed the obligation to seek and tell 'the whole truth and nothing but the truth.' The results you supply are part of that commitment.

You know, Dr. Nyhan, my brothers and I grew up believing that doctors were gods, not only because our dad was a pediatrician, but because in that era, you guys (and all of you were guys!) were supposed to be infallible. A heavy burden, I'm sure, and one that clearly weighed on our father when he could not help his own son.

My goodness, how the years have changed our perspective about doctors and medicine! Looking back, it seems incredible that I failed to question my gynecologist further about his claim that my fourteenth week of gestation was "too late for amniocentesis," or that I did not query David on the reliability of the test that indicated my carrier status. But in the context of our time, each of us did the best we could with the information available to us.

I honestly have no regrets. My family and I have been extraordinarily blessed. For me, it all began by growing up with our extraordinary little brother Bob.

Sincerely,
Anne

Afterword

About More Recent Developments Affecting the
Sunland Residents and Other Americans with Disabilities

Standing behind every superhero are those ordinary people working to secure the rights of the disenfranchised. For America's children with disabilities, they were the hundreds of thousands of parents who advocated on behalf of their children, many inspired by the African-American struggle for civil rights. Some became plaintiffs in landmark court decisions such as *The Pennsylvania Association for Retarded Citizens v. Commonwealth* (1971) and *Mills v. Board of Education of the District of Columbia* (1972), which established the states' responsibility to educate children with disabilities and led to the federal Education for All Handicapped Children Act of 1975.

Four years after the original version of the Individuals with Disabilities Education Act (IDEA) was signed into law, the Florida Legislature finally required our public schools to enroll and serve the hundreds of school-aged residents of the six Sunland institutions. By then, Leon County Public Schools were already serving every school-aged child at Tallahassee Sunland Hospital, and the small teaching staff at Tallahassee Sunland served all our adult residents. We were immensely proud to be the first Sunland to reach that goal.

Tallahassee Sunland Hospital closed its doors in 1983; Orlando Sunland Hospital closed in 1985. Many residents from these two hospitals were moved to Medicaid-funded residences known as Intermediate Care Facilities for the Developmentally Disabled (ICF/DD), where the school-aged residents were enrolled in local public school programs. To facilitate these closures, the State of Florida constructed sixteen Cluster Homes, each comprised of three co-located houses serving eight residents apiece in a homelike setting, remarkably similar to the Gatchell School, albeit operated under strict federal requirements. The transfer of so many medically fragile residents did not proceed without significant setbacks to the residents' health and safety, including some deaths. (O'Neall, Foster, and Butler 1984)

The Gatchell School in Decatur, Georgia, continued as a residence for individuals with severe developmental disabilities until 2005. The property at 1458 Holly Lane, originally purchased primarily by the Mills Lane family, now houses Yeshiva Ohr Yisrael, a small high school for Jewish boys. Funds from the property's sale went to the Holly Lane Foundation, which continues to distribute funds to nonprofit organizations serving people with neuromuscular and severe developmental disabilities as well as brain injuries.

About Our Family and Careers

Mother (Joanna Law Martin) and Julia Hillman corresponded for decades after Bob's death, especially at Christmastime. Mother found deep solace in the kind words of the woman who had earned meager wages caring for Bob as though he were her own son.

After our father (Dr. D. W. Martin) served as chief-of-staff and director of medical education at St. Mary's Hospital in West Palm Beach, he became director of pediatric care and health officer for the Palm Beach County Health Department where he promoted immunization programs and established a seizure clinic. He co-founded Healthy Mothers-Healthy Babies of Palm Beach, a nonprofit organization that provides access to prenatal care for underserved and uninsured pregnant women.

My brother David (Dr. D. W. Martin Jr.) served as chief of UCSF Department of Medicine's Medical Genetics Services from 1970 to 1982. Subsequently, he was senior vice-president of research and development at Genentech (1982–1990); executive vice-president of research and development at DuPont Merck (1991–1993); president of Chiron Therapeutics (1994–1995); and founder and CEO of Eos Biotechnology (1997–2003). He founded and currently serves as CEO of AvidBiotics Corporation, a privately held and privately funded biotherapeutic company that develops non-antibody proteins, specifically targeting bacteria, viruses, or cancer cells for human therapeutic and prophylactic uses as well as food safety and biodefense. See www.avidbiotics.com. David's wife, Kathy McKinnon Martin, RN, MFA, continues to serve as her twin sister's legal guardian, overseeing her care in a special group residence.

Following my eight years at Tallahassee Sunland Hospital, I worked at Florida State University in the arena of prevention of disabilities and early intervention. I coordinated the services of Panhandle Healthy Start, a federally funded home-visiting program for expectant families aimed at reducing infant mortality. Through weekly home visits, our registered nurses and paraprofessional staff offered guidance to families whose infants had an elevated risk of dying or developing a disability. After working with so many individuals who had intractable conditions, I found it refreshing to help new families insulate their infants from potential harm through good nutrition, medical care, and attentive nurturing.

With lessons learned from our federal Healthy Start project, I co-authored, with my FSU colleagues, a home visitor's training curriculum known as *Partners for a Healthy Baby*. The curriculum is used by more than twelve hundred programs throughout Florida and other states, including New York, Tennessee, Ohio, Virginia, and Oregon. See www.cpeip.fsu.edu.

About Lesch-Nyhan Syndrome
(Edited by Dr. Nyhan, August 2012)

Lesch-Nyhan syndrome (LNS) is a rare, genetic disorder caused by mutations in the HPRT gene on the X chromosome. Sometimes called Lesch-Nyhan disease, it is an X-linked recessive trait, a condition passed by a carrier mother to her son. The condition occurs rarely in females.

Individuals with LNS have delayed and abnormal motor development, often initially diagnosed as cerebral palsy. Their bodies have a deficiency of the enzyme hypoxanthine-guanine phosphoribosyltransferase (HGPRTase), resulting in overproduction of uric acid and, absent treatment, a severe form of gout. Individuals with LNS tend to be alert and socially engaging, but have cognitive disabilities in the mild to moderate range. The hallmark behavior of LNS is self-injury, particularly biting their hands and lips. Individuals may display other compulsive or impulsive behaviors sometimes interpreted as aggressive or manipulative.

The reported prevalence of Lesch-Nyhan syndrome is 1 in 380,000 persons worldwide, with roughly equal rates for most ethnicities. Definitive diagnosis of LNS is made by assay of the enzyme. Genetic decision-making is aided by identifying a molecular mutation in the gene known as HGPRT1, which was cloned and sequenced in 1985. Molecular genetic diagnosis (DNA analysis) is the ideal tool for detecting carriers of Lesch-Nyhan and for prenatal screening of at-risk pregnancies. The auto-radiographic technique used by Dr. Seegmiller in the 1970s to determine carrier status was found to be unreliable and is no longer used for this purpose.

The uric acid overproduction in LNS patients is treatable, but few treatments for the neurologic and behavioral difficulties are available. Individuals with the syndrome seldom survive their third or fourth decade. Sudden unexpected death is common.

In the late 1980s, Lesch-Nyhan syndrome was considered one of the conditions for which gene therapy (replacing the defective gene of a genetic disease with an intact version of that gene) held great promise (Schmeck 1986). My brother David, who at that time served on the National Institutes of Health's Recombinant DNA Advisory Committee, reports that the gene therapy arena in general has been partially successful, the first successful therapy being for adenosine deaminase (ADA) deficiency in children (think "immuno-deficient Bubble Boy"). More recently, there have been successful studies in other immuno deficiencies and certain forms of blindness as well as effective treatment of hemophilia B (Wade 2011), but for Lesch-Nyhan syndrome, the promise of gene therapy has so far not panned out. David indicates the challenge for Lesch-Nyhan is that the blood-brain barrier probably has to be breached to generate effective gene therapy.

For more information about current research and Lesch-Nyhan syndrome, please consult www.ninds.nih.gov and www.emedicine. com. A network for those living with the disorder, their families, teachers, and other interested people can be found at lndnet.ning. com. This website, created by Lowell T. Anderson PhD, serves as an important and much appreciated source of ongoing support to parents.

About the Highly Personal Matters of Prenatal Diagnosis, Pregnancy Termination, and Adoption

Four decades since my flight to San Francisco, prenatal screening and diagnostic tests are increasingly common. Advances in genetic medicine and prenatal genetic diagnosis have brought more reliable procedures that can be performed earlier and more safely to help parents assess or reduce their risk of having a child with a genetic anomaly.

For pregnant women who have an increased risk of having an infant with a genetic disorder or who are known carriers, the prenatal diagnostic procedure known as chorionic villus sampling (called "CVS" in Tania Salkind's letter below) can determine whether a fetus has a chromosomal defect at ten to twelve weeks of pregnancy, rather than waiting for amniocentesis, commonly performed during or after the fifteenth week of pregnancy.

A highly technical (not to mention controversial and extraordinarily expensive) embryo-screening procedure, known as pre-implantation genetic diagnosis (PGD) is now available to enable known carriers of serious inheritable conditions who want to plan a pregnancy, to successfully avoid producing a baby affected by that condition. With PGD, a couple's embryos are created outside the womb using *in vitro* fertilization and tested for a genetic disorder before implanting a few selected embryos in the womb.

For most parents, the experience of testing and deciding remains a harrowing one, as evidenced by my electronic conversation with Tania Salkind, whom I met on an international website for families living with Lesch-Nyhan syndrome (www.lndnet.ning.com). She and I "talked" as I was preparing my manuscript for publication and suddenly had cold feet about publicly sharing the details of my personal experience. Tania had identified herself as the mother of two sons with Lesch-Nyhan and a daughter who was a confirmed Lesch-Nyhan carrier. When I asked for her thoughts on the topic of therapeutic/elective abortion, her response gave me the courage I needed to proceed. With her permission, I include her warm and lovely electronic message, dated February 4, 2012:

> Hi Anne,
>
> I am willing to share any thoughts that my daughter and I have on this difficult subject.
>
> Her pregnancy was unplanned. It was difficult from the start, as she was twenty-two, still lived at home with us, had no money, and her boyfriend was in the same situation. These were hurdles that could be overcome with the support of their families. Obviously the most worrying thing was that she knew she was a

carrier of LN (she chose to find out her carrier status when she was sixteen).

Luckily, she found out she was pregnant very early on. There is now a test that they can do from about six weeks that can determine the sex of the baby. This is a simple blood test, but the results took a couple of weeks to come back as it is quite specialized, and had to go to a research lab in London. As you can imagine, we were really hoping that she was having a girl, and the wait for the results was excruciating. When she got the call telling her the baby was a boy, she was devastated (as were we all) as she knew the baby had a 50/50 chance of having LN. She also knew that she would have to go through the unpleasant process of CVS.

My daughter has always said that if any baby she carried had LN that she would terminate the pregnancy. This is something that we all agreed would be the right thing to do and that she would have our full support. Like you, she was extremely close to her brothers, Luke and Alfie, particularly Alfie, as she was only three when Luke died, and was fifteen when Alfie died. Alfie was the light of her life; she was more than a big sister, she was also a little caregiver to him, and they were extraordinarily close. The boys (as most LN kids seem to be!) were clever, adorable, and so so funny; they were universally loved by all who knew them. However, my daughter has seen how much they suffered, and she said she would never knowingly bring a child into the world to suffer pain. Also, having been through the devastating pain of losing the boys, she could not go through having a child that would more than likely die before she did. These are the reasons she would have had an abortion.

The CVS process was awful, and the one week wait for the results seemed like ten years, but [the moment] when she took the call saying the baby was healthy and free of LN rates as one of the best of our lives! There were lots more tears, but this time of joy! She is due to give birth on March first, and we cannot wait! [She] and her boyfriend have just moved into their own home, which was a wrench for me, but it's only a three-minute drive, and I still see her almost every day. I know she wants more than one child, so this is a process she may have to go through again, but we will cross that bridge when we come to it!! In the meantime, we'll celebrate having a healthy boy in our family!

Just a little more background info on me, I am the only carrier of LN in my family (apart from my daughter), so the gene must have mutated in me. I have two sisters that are unaffected, and my mum wasn't a carrier. My son Luke died when he was twenty months old. He died suddenly of pneumonia, and I found him dead in his cot. He was never diagnosed with LN; we just thought he had cerebral palsy. A year after he died, I got pregnant with Alfie, not knowing I was the carrier of a genetic condition. Having already had a disabled child, I knew near enough immediately there was something wrong with him just by the way he was feeding. Of course, I was treated like a paranoid mother, but they finally took me seriously when he was about five months old. However, they didn't have any diagnosis for him, and when he was about two-and-a-half, he started punching himself constantly in the nose. We took him to ENT specialists as we thought there was something wrong with his nose! We saw many doctors, and still no diagnosis! I thought he might have a psychological problem, so asked that he be referred to a hospital that specializes in children with mental illness and psych problems, and I finally got some answers! By this time, he was almost five and had a huge hole under his lips. From then on, he was referred also to great Ormond Street Hospital, which is a world-famous children's hospital, and I started to get all the help and equipment he needed. Alfie died suddenly in his sleep when he was nine. He was not at all sick; it was just a sudden death, and I found him dead in his bed in the morning.

If I had the choices that my daughter has now, I would make the same decisions as she has, for the same reasons. That does not mean I didn't love my boys. I loved them with all my heart and do still, and I miss them every day, even after eighteen and seven yrs. However, I am glad that they do not have to suffer anymore.

I hope I have been helpful and answered your questions. Please feel free to ask me anything you want. I don't get to talk about them much anymore, and I'm quite enjoying doing so!

Best wishes,
Tania xx

Neil Genzlinger, a writer for *The New York Times* and parent of a daughter with Rett syndrome, has called therapeutic abortion "the emerging…moral dilemma of our time." Anecdotal evidence I encountered while researching this book (in addition to Tania's story) assures me that the *emerging* phase is over, the dilemma in full bloom.

The unpublicized truth is that every day, across the world, couples with prenatal genetic diagnoses decide where to draw the line between accepting "the natural diversity of human beings" versus preventing a serious disability. Studies have consistently reported that ninety percent of women with fetal diagnoses of Down syndrome—often a relatively mild condition—end their pregnancies. Vocal parents of individuals with Down syndrome have expressed concern about the dwindling Down syndrome population (Harmon 2007).

Genetic counselors have become widely available to help parents understand their risk and make the best decision they can for themselves and their families. A decade ago, one study reported that women who received genetic counseling said they weren't given information about future quality-of-life issues for individuals with disabilities, nor were they given the positive as well as the negative aspects of giving birth to a child with disabilities (Roberts 2002). Since that criticism surfaced, The National Society of Genetic Counselors has worked to help genetic counseling students as well as the organization's 2,600 members gain the insight and skills to provide patients and families with a balanced view of inheritable conditions, including developmental disabilities. The NSGC's December 2012 special edition on developmental disabilities (including portions of this memoir) is part of the organization's ongoing commitment to address this challenge.

Nevertheless, each couple's (or individual's) decision is molded not only by the advice they receive, but also by their own deeply held beliefs about disabilities, illness, religion, science, and medicine. No wonder we hear such wide and vehement disagreement about what the better—or less worse—decision would be. We can only hope that medical scientists will soon discover ways to move beyond the *in utero detection* of devastating inheritable diseases like Lesch-Nyhan to *curing* them.

While I respect those who make the opposite decision from what I made, I have never regretted my own. I do regret that so many who face this decision do so without comprehending the important benefits so many children with developmental disabilities bring to their families. When faced with my own dilemma, I was fully cognizant of the many ways that Bob and his disability had enriched my life and that of my family. I also knew what Lesch-Nyhan syndrome does to little boys.

Hugh and I were fortunate in that we already had two wonderful little ones. We divorced approximately four years later, but it worked out well for us. We each promptly remarried and have remained friends, sharing our grandchildren and living a few doors down the street from each other.

Since I spent most of my adult life convinced I was a carrier for Bob's condition, I was lucky that my father's role in numerous newborn adoptions had given me a positive view of adoption. I would encourage others who face similar obstacles to parenthood to embrace the beautiful, win-win solution of adoption.

All across the U.S. (not only on the other side of the world), babies and children wait to be loved by a parent or two. Of course, nothing about having kids is simple. Those who need a home may not share your ethnicity, they may have passed the age you were hoping for, or have some type of disability, or even need to bring their siblings along. For these reasons, couples and individuals who adopt tend to face the same questions faced by those with difficult prenatal diagnoses: How far from our expectations and our family culture can we accept? Since every child brings both burden and blessing, how might raising this particular child affect us and our family?

My new husband and I contemplated these questions back in 1983 when we decided to adopt a third child, an adorable and active five-month-old boy who didn't look a heck of a lot like us, but who would soon run and play like other children and have a crack at living long enough to take his place in the adult world. Like his siblings Sarah and Hugh Bob, our son Martin is grown now and working to make this world a better place.

WORKS CITED

Bavar, Emily. 1972. "Sunland Probe Ends, Report Awaited." *Orlando Sentinel*, February 14.

Harmon, Amy. 2007. "Prenatal Test Puts Down Syndrome in Hard Focus." *New York Times*, May 9.

Individuals with Disabilities Education Act (IDEA). 1981. 20 U.S.C., Sec. 1400 Congressional statements and declarations.

Firestein, Stuart. 2012. *Ignorance: How It Drives Science*. New York: Oxford University Press.

Lawrence, D. G. 1972a. "Judges Kill Florida's Old Abortion Law." *Palm Beach Post,* February 15.

———. 1972b. "Sunland Overhaul Ordered." *Orlando Sentinel*, February 16.

———. 1972c. "Gunter's Plea: $998,750 to Help Sunland Hospital." *Orlando Sentinel*, March 28.

——— and T. Twitty. 1971. "New Criticism Aimed at Sunland Hospital. *Orlando Sentinel*, December 30.

Moreno-De-Lucaa, Andres, David Ledbetter, and Christa Martin. 2012. "Genetic Insights into the Causes and Classification of the Cerebral Palsies." *The Lancet Neurology*. 11 (3): 283–292.

O'Neall, Linda, Ray Foster, and Beth Butler. 1984. "The Hodges Report." Tallahassee, FL: Brehon Institute for Human Services.

Reid, D. 1971. "Alachua Abortions Legal?" *Orlando Sentinel,* December 14.

Roberts, Christy D., Laura M. Stough, and Linda H. Parrish. 2002. "The Role of Genetic Counseling in the Elective Termination of Pregnancies Involving Fetuses with Disabilities." *The Journal of Special Education.* 36 (1): 48-55.

Schillinger, Liesl. 2011. "With or Without You." Review of *Portrait of a Marriage* by Sándor Márai. *New York Times Sunday Book Review,* February 27.

Schmeck, Harold M., Jr. 1986. "Hereditary Disease: New Therapies Are Closer." *New York Times*, January 28.

Seegmiller, J. Edwin. 1972. "Lesch-Nyhan Syndrome and the X-linked Uric Acidurias." *Hospital Practice.* 7 (4): 79–90.

Stone, Ellen. 1972. "Hodes Calls Sunland Program Humane." *Orlando Sentinel*, January 1.

United Cerebral Palsy. 2008. "UCP: Press Room – Vocabulary Tips" http://www.ucp.org/ucp_generaldoc.cfm/1/9/37/37-37/447.

U.S. Department of Education. 2007. "Conditions before IDEA" in *Special Education & Rehabilitative Services. Archived: A 25 Year History of the IDEA*. http://www2.ed.gov/policy/speced/leg/idea/history.html.

Wade, Nicholas. 2011. "Treatment for Blood Disease Is Gene Therapy Landmark." *New York Times,* December 10.

Acknowledgements

Portions of this memoir were published in slightly different form in the December 2012 issue of *The Journal of Genetic Counseling*. Thanks to the National Society of Genetic Counselors for their permission to reprint it here.

I thank my brother David and his wife Kathy McKinnon Martin of Mill Valley, California, for sharing their recollection of David's 1966 discovery about Bob's condition and for David's crucial help in explaining the genetic and medical details of our family's story. Without his help, I would not have dared tackle this project.

I thank Carmen Ramos for allowing me to use her beautiful, original artwork "Flamingos" for the background of the collage on the cover of this book. Carmen and I first met decades ago when she was a brown-eyed, curly-haired, little girl at Tallahassee Sunland Hospital. A wheelchair dancer as well as visual artist, she produced this work in collaboration with her art instructor at Pyramid, Inc.

The following individuals reviewed my manuscript, in whole or in part, and offered invaluable help: William L. Nyhan, MD, PhD, at the University of California at San Diego's Biochemical Genetics Laboratory; Jan Goddard-Finegold, MD, pediatric neurologist in Houston, Texas; Tom Zavelson, MD, retired pediatrician in Gainesville, Florida; Rebecca R. Fewell, PhD, retired professor of pediatrics, University of Miami School of Medicine; Louise Reid Ritchie, PhD, Tallahassee; Jon Weil, PhD, Associate Clinical Professor of Pediatrics, UC San Francisco, former director of the Program in Genetic Counseling, UC Berkeley (1989-2001), and author of *Psychosocial Genetic Counseling*, Oxford University Press 2000; Jeanne McDermott, author of *Babyface: A Story of Heart and Bones* and science teacher in Cambridge, MA; Carol Ward Wilson, author of *A Handful of Rain*; Dexter and Kurt, devoted fathers of boys with Lesch-Nyhan syndrome; Rita LeBlanc and Joan Patterson from the Center for Prevention & Early Intervention at Florida State University, Tallahassee; and my dear friend, Fita Ferguson, who set her own writing aside to help me with mine.

Editor Marsha Butler of *Take Flight* Literary Services saved me from a plague of errors, dumb decisions, and rule-breaking mischief in my manuscript; those that remain are my own bullheaded fault. Mike Butler of Michael by Design extracted me from the cruel jaws of self-publishing hell by tweaking the photographs and book cover I wanted, and formatting my final manuscript for publication. Thank you both for the rescue.

I will be forever grateful to my "village" of former colleagues at FSU as well as friends and neighbors who hunted answers to my questions, loaned me their eyes, ears, and cameras, and cheered me on.

Most importantly, I thank my husband—my love, my life—for his endless (well, almost) patience, especially on those evenings when he came home to find me still in morning exercise garb, glued to my laptop, my face puffy and red from rekindled grief for the brother I lost. One glance, and he'd offer, "Let's order takeout!"